The New Volunteerism

THE NEW VOLUNTEERISM
A Community Connection

by

Barbara Feinstein

and

Catherine Cavanaugh

Library of Congress Number: 76-7838

ISBN: 87073-780-5 *cloth*
87073-781-3 *paper*

Printed in the United States of America

DEDICATION

To our husbands and best friends . . .
Herb Feinstein and Mike Cavanaugh

To Barbara's daughters, Lisa and Debbie, who are her most devoted fans . . .

Thank you for the love and inspiration that you give us.

TABLE OF CONTENTS

Foreword

Louis Lowy, MS in S.S., PH D
Professor of Social Work, Boston University

"Volunteers have always been an integral part of the American scene. Professionalization of the helping services and specialization have at times seemed to diminish their importance. In each period, however, voices have been raised to indicate that we were involved with changing patterns rather than elimination.—Cohen, Nathan E., ed. The Citizen Volunteer, p. xiii.

The 1960's have been a period when such voices have been raised again and when volunteering took on a new meaning for many people. During that period, a redefinition of volunteerism has taken place in the social welfare field. Generally a volunteer has been defined as an individual who contributes his/her services to a cause or organization without remuneration. In a new definition, the phrase "without remuneration" has been modified to include: "commensurate with the value of the services rendered", and before long the term "para-professional" appeared, denoting that this person so designated assists "professionals" in carrying out their particular functions, sometimes with pay, sometimes without pay. The line of demarcation between volunteers and para-professionals has not been neatly drawn, and in many instances, the original definition of a volunteer as a person performing a task without pay has been amended to include a person performing a task at a minimal pay. Increasingly, para-professionals, such as case-aides in the human services fields, have become accepted as service providers who aid full-fledged professionals to carry out specific tasks.

As a result of a recognition of the myriad contributions which para-professionals, paid or unpaid, have made in the last decade, social workers as well as other human service professionals have come to accept and respect these contributions, and in fact have moved towards delimiting various levels of practice by task differentiation. The National Association of Social Workers has moved towards such a categorization with specification of levels of practice by complexity of task, and requisite training for each level[1], and Frank Reissman has conceptualized the role of the new non-professional and has related this role to new career patterns for individuals within the context of their contributions to service as para-professionals.[2] Willard Richan evolved a theoretical scheme for determining roles of professional and non-professional personnel predicated upon worker autonomy on the one hand and client vulnerability on the other.[3] He pointed out that when worker autonomy and client vulnerability are high, the "pure" professional would be called for, while para-professionals such as case-aides would come into play when client vulnerability and worker autonomy were relatively low. Although this scheme is an over-simplification, it has provided a theoretical handle to differentiate levels of practice and to guide standards for training. Meanwhile, data have shown that a complement of full professionals, para-professionals and non-professionals have particular know-how, expertise and skills that they can bring to bear upon social problems and conditions which need change or amelioration.[4] Consequently, the role of full professionals has become redefined, and their tasks now include a heavy dse of training and supervision of para-professionals or volunteers. Since professionals and para-professionals have functioned as members of teams, all parties had to learn the role of being team-members.

This book tells the story of a new volunteerism. It presents a graphic description of the rise and fall of a case-aide program in a mental hospital, of the emptiness of a mental hospital, of the sense of despair of its patients and the void in the lives of those who live and work there. However, this book is not only confined to a description of thc hospital, thc program and ty people involved, but also deptics the milieu and the ups and downs of events, and demonstrates that a case-aide program *did* work. The story presented bears witness to a highly motivated force of volunteers who have reaped psychic rewards for meaningful jobs well done.

This report demonstrates further that a case-aide program needs a philosophy which was simply stated as "the job of the case-aides have acted in accord with this philosophy and that relationships, felt, communicated, and conveyed, are a powerful tool in channelling despair into hope. As long as human beings can communicate and show that they care for each other, they will benefit from this encounter.

What else can we learn from this project?

(1) Professionals do not have to hie their lack of omnipotence. On the contrary, they strengthen non-professionals in their sense of security by freely admitting their own limitations. (2) The extent of influence by professionals can be increased by an appreciable ration through the judicious use of para-professionals/volunteers and many problems that demand the services of a caring human being are closer to resolution when such caring human beings are available. (3) What case-aides need, such as a sense of reality, a skill to establish, maintain and terminate relationships, and resourcefulness, apply to all human service workers. (4) Supervision is effective as a practice method of telescoping expertise, experience and know-how through various professional levels to the consumers of the services. The chapter dealing with this subject is appropriately called "The Backbone—Supervision". Here the authors describe the use of five types of supervision and delineate the appropriateness of each type for particular purposes. They argue for a combination of these five types (individual supervision, group supervision, peer supervision, co-therapy, and co-supervision); regardless of types used, the authors make a powerful case that only through competent supervision by professionals can case-aides achieve the service goals. (5) We learn much about the conditions under which work with groups rather than with individid-

uals alone became a preferred stance of practice; case-aides in fact become group-aides. This chapter provides valuable information on the training of volunteer group leaders; it also demonstrates the effectiveness of this modality in working with the mentally ill, especially those who have been institutionalized. It might serve as a model for the development of other volunteer group-work services with such populations as: the blind, the retarded, the physically handicapped, etc. As a result, the nomenclature is in need of revision to encompass work with individuals and groups. (6) A chapter modestly tucked away towards the end of the book teaches us quite a bit about organizational and structural variables of the mental institution and how these have impinged upon the development, operation and termination of this program.

The book has stimulated me to raise a few issues which should be addressed in the social welfare field with regard to the use of the new volunteer:

(1) The hiatus of status between professionals and para-professionals is more than a matter of feeling or affect; it is as much a power issue evolving in a status-conscious society. In addition, it is an issue closely related to the lack of precise definitions of functions of service givers in the mental health and social service fields. However, instead of becoming obsessed with arriving at sharp demarcation lines, it may be more fruitful to specify tasks to be performed and to inventorize competencies available in order to match them in offering best possible services to cleints and patients. (2) Another issue revolves around the use of volunteers in such a way that they do not become substitutes for inadequately remunerated workers. In other words, volunteers should not become a cover-up for labor exploitation. (3) Working contracts have to be made not only between para-professionals and professionals, but also between agency policy makers and administrators on the one hand, and between administrators and direct service providers on the other. (4) Another issue relates to training and supervision; to what extent is imparting of knowledge and information a function of supervision and to what extent is it a function of a comprehensive training program of which supervision constitutes a significant part? (5) How can volunteers particupate in bringing about changes in a system that is inimical to the well-being of the patients?

What is the role of the professional in enabling volunteers to become change agents rather than officials who perform adjustmental functions. An extension of the professional service system through the use of para-professionals, paid or unpaid, can lead to a firming up on an undesirable status quo and therefore work against organizational or other systems changes, when these are called for instead.

The American heritage of volunteerism has created an enormous amount of benefits which have accrued to the volunteers themselves as well as to those on whose behalf volunteers have worked. The strengths and the positive effects as well as the inspiring lessons learned in the saga of volunteerism are a tribute to this American heritage. On the other hand, volunteerism could also be used to justify in our society a lack of action on the part of appropriate governmental agencies and to circumvent federal, state and local machinery to deal with social problems and to provide the essential funding for paid service providers. In other words, we have to strike a balance in direct services provisions with unpaid/paid para-professionals (volunteers) and "full" professionals. Otherwise, an over-relaince on volunteers without adequate backup of fully trained people paid for in a cash-oriented society could lead to a further depletion of the quality, if not quantity, of social services. For this reason, it is imperative to study systematically the role and use of volunteers, the impact of volunteerism upon the volunteer and clients, and the differential contributions made by them in the social welfare field. This is essential to guide manpower policies as well as to design training programs and to harness the latent strengths and motivations of people who desire to translate their humanitarian ethos into significant social action.

In this world of ours, we are always faced with trade-offs. Professionalization has led to increased knowledge, more predictable, equitable performances, and in the human services fields to a greater institutionalized rather than residual conceptualization of social welfare. As the same time, it has also led to a decrease of humanitarian caring and warmth, of spontaneity and an emphasis of vertical rather than horizontal relationships. Obviously, a healthy mix of the strengths that professionalism has brought and the strengths inherent in volunteerism should be combined. Our ingenuity must be challenged to search for modes of such mixing. This book grapples with the issues I have raised by implication and inference. As such, it sets the stage for further discussions that should ensue following its publication. The authors have made a great contribution not only by "telling it like it is", but also be "telling it like it might be." Towards this end, this volume is a significant contribution to the social welfare literature.

1. *NASW Standards for Social Work Personnel Practices,* NASW Policy Pamphlets, Pub. No. JPP-802-F.

2. Frank Reissman, "The Revolution in Social Work: The New Non-Professional", Mobilization for Youth, New York, 1963; and Frank Reissman; Albert Cohen; Arthur Pearl; *Mental Health for the Poor,* Free Press, 1964.

3. Willard C. Richan, "A Theoretical Scheme for Determining Roles" in *Social Work,* vol. 6, no. 4, 1961, pp. 22-28.

4. Donald Brieland; Thomas Briggs; Paul Leuenberger; *The Team Model of Social Work Practice,* Syracuse Univ. Press, Syracuse, N.Y., 1973, p. 5.

ACKNOWLEDGMENTS

Our love and concern for our clients—the patients in the mental institution that employed us—and our love for and pride in the many wonderful men and women who worked with us as case aides inspired us to take our experiences and to turn them into a concrete and constructive book so that others could share with us and learn with us.

There will be many who will read this book and recall their own experiences as case aides in our program or in other programs. We are reminded of the woman who rode her bicycle six miles to volunteer, of another who hitchhiked from a college ten miles away . . . and of so many others who gave so much of themselves to help the mentally ill in this particular hospital. We hope that they will accept this book as our "thank you".

One of the people who most exemplified the case aide spirit was herself a case aide for four years. She is also the person who typed and helped to edit the manuscript: Joan Morgan. Her suggestions and comments have been incorporated into this book and we are very grateful that she took the time, in spite of a job and her family, to help us; it was truly a labor of love.

It may sound trite, but it is nonetheless true that, without our families—parents, parents-in-law, brothers and sisters, as well as husbands and children, to whom this book is dedicated—we could not have persevered in this long and demanding, exciting and satisfying project.

Thank you also to our publisher, Alfred Schenkman, who saw a glimmer of something valuable and special in our first crude and incomplete manuscript and who gave us the opportunity and time to rewrite this book.

We are grateful to each other for nagging one another when one or the other of us grew tired, bored, or lazy. Somehow, we miraculously have remained friends and respectful colleagues throughout this long and difficult year.

And, perhaps most of all, we would like to acknowledge the courage and hard work of the many patients who made use of the service that we had to offer. The case aides may have provided the necessary key to open the door, but it was the individual patient—alone and afraid—who walked through.

PREFACE

It is our hope that by describing and analyzing the strengths and weaknesses of a particular volunteer program, at a state mental hospital, we will provide a body of knowledge for other professionals and for other administrators who may be working with volunteers. It is our hope also that the great unmet need for human services will be answered by the emergence of dozens of volunteer programs, all of them well organized and effective, which would extend the reach of our professional arms. And, it is our hope finally that capable and caring individuals and groups will be given here ammunition for helping others while they themselves learn and grow.

Barbara Baroff Feinstein
Catherine Catterson Cavanaugh

INTRODUCTION

The two authors have written this book based on their experiences as two social workers employed at a state mental hospital. It is not their purpose to write a sensational expose. Their book could easily have become such an expose since they saw, first hand, the terrible conditions, the pervading apathy, and the awesome waste of our fellow men. Such exposes elicit much horrified noise, but little constructive action; this is mainly because most people simply do not know what to do about these tales of misery. In addition, the large mental hospital is becoming obsolete as a service delivery form and does not deserve any more attention and validation than it has already received.

The New Volunteerism is, instead, about a program that really worked, that made a significant impact on one hospital's population. There are several reasons for writing the story. The program, the Case Aide Program, helped over 400 patients to leave the hospital and to pick up their lives again. In spite of this success, the Program was killed. We want its story told.

The authors also feel a responsibility to share with others how they set up and operated such an effective and economical service. At its height, 120 patients were seen weekly using only two paid staff persons. Rarely, if ever, does information appear about the administration of service oriented projects. There is a great deal written on psychological, sociological, or theoretical levels with no concrete or technical data on the organization and on-going operation of programs. Actually, the vast majority of service organizations are administered by "professionals" who may or may not be competent to perform the service that their agency provides, but who may not have any administrative or managerial expertise. Somehow, this aspect is deemed unimportant and yet the result is the wasting of millions of tax dollars.

There are statements made in this book about the current status of the mentally ill, albeit based on somewhat limited experiences, and only with the New England area. The experiences described here, however, were a microcosm of what we believe is happening inside institutions throughout the country. There is a general shifting of philosophy, populations, and funds from isolated, large hospitals to smaller, community-based agencies. This shift spotlights the gaps in human services and resources. One resource that has tremendous untapped potential for plugging the gaps is the volunteer. A well trained, well supervised volunteer operating within a viable program can function as an adjunct to the professional. Limited funding and the dearth of qualified manpower heightens the attractiveness of the volunteer paraprofessional

The New Volunteerism evolved out of a year's thinking, re-thinking, writing and re-writing, defining and re-defining, living and re-living the pain, anger, and frustration of the precipitous end of a program that was creative, dynamic, sensitive, and effective. The various drafts reflected different emotional stages of separation and termination. The first stage was begun in anger and was a tirade against the insanity and self-destructive qualities of the institutional system; as time passed, the authors gained some degree of perspective and were more able to see that there were elements of the program worth abstracting. In spite of particular difficulties within one system, the program model is generalizable. We feel that it can be effectively utilized especially in the interface between institutions and communities, and within the communities themselves.

As may be partly apparent in reading this volume, *The New Volunteerism* is the result of two social workers working together, between New York and Boston, each bringing to it a peculiar style, personality, and opinions. Some chapters were written predominantly by one of the authors; others are a conglomerate of the thoughts of both.

The New Volunteerism

CHAPTER I
"WILL YOU OPEN THE DOOR FOR ME?"

THE PROGRAM

"Will you open the door for me?"

"Oh God!" I thought, "can I ever remember which of these keys opens this door?" There are two years worth of accumulated junk in my pocketbook . . . at the bottom, of course . . . fiddle with the antiquated lock . . . "Of course I'll open it for you. What's your name?"

"Mary," she whispers.

"Pleased to meet you, Mary." (It does not occur to Mary to give her last name. She lost her individual identity a long time ago.) "My name is Barbara. Have you ever heard of the Case Aide Program?"

And so, off we went trying to open another and much more important door for Mary, the one leading her back into the world as a functioning woman.

Who were these door openers and why and how did they open it? They were an organization of volunteer paraprofessionals in the Case Aide Program who attempted to alleviate the isolation, the despair, and the loneliness of the patients in one state mental hospital.

Mental patients—cut off from the world by their illness or their circumstances—need assistance coping with the myriad of "nitty-gritty" problems that must be dealt with before they can even begin to think about a life outside the hospital's walls.

The purpose of the Case Aide Program was to provide such assistance by helping the patient reacclimate himself to the "straight" world. It was our conviction that, with such personal help, many patients now living a "death-in-life" inside our mental institutions could make it out and stay there. Achieving this end would, in our opinion, have two immediate advantages. Firstly, life for the person who is not openly psychotic is better on the outside than in; secondly, it is enormously less wasteful of our resources—both human and financial—to have them as contributing members of society than to have inmates in state supported institutions where the longer they stay, the more likely it is that they will stay longer.

In order to make the actual operation of the Case Aide Program intelligible, it is necessary to describe the context in which it operated. Observed within the hospital setting, the reason for its effectiveness in spirit, goals, and philosophy becomes glaringly apparent.

THE PHYSICAL SETTING

The hospital in which the Case Aide Program operated was located among several suburban, prosperous communities. Viewed from the road, the hospital's landscape is perfectly in keeping with the lovely homes and gardens common to the area. The drive past the superintendent's lovely Tudor-styled estate with its white bell tower reveals carefully manicured lawns that are not to be walked on, newly painted garden furniture that is not to be sat on, and masses of multicolored flowers that are not to be picked.

All this external beauty does not prepare you for the squalid patients' living quarters within. And an even worse contrast are the poorly clad, hopeless human beings whose shuffling procession intrudes upon the idyllic scene.

While acute patients and staff are housed in the more modern buildings that are easily accessible to the public, the "chronics" exist within the masses of red brick and iron fencing that make up the twenty-four ward compound that is "home" to 1,000 former human beings, now called patients. As a visitor, your first introduction to the inside of the hospital is a paint-flaked, smelly lobby, filled to overflowing with over-drugged and under-utilized patients. Urine and feces are winning their thirty-five year old battle with dirty mops and disinfectant. The temperature is either hot enough to put you to sleep or cold enough to give you chilblains. A pot of artificial flowers and a gay red Coke machine distinguish this as one of the more attractive and welcoming places in the entire compound.

Access to the wards from this lobby is blocked by locked doors. Large, jangly, heavy metal, four-inch-long keys are door openers in every sense. If you have the keys, all else falls into place. They distinguish the good guys from the bad, the powerful from the weak, the sane from the crazy.

And up you climb . . . wired windows . . . stairs pitted and crusted . . . dirt and human waste . . . dark and dank . . . breathing the smell of misery and fear . . . unlock the door on the next floor . . . onto the ward and dayhall . . . the patient watering hole . . . chairs, wooden and crooked, lined up along the narrow corridors . . . more wired windows . . . more plastic flowers looking gray with age and weariness . . . a clock with hands that never move . . . a television blaring its mechanical message that patients, sitting in stony silence, do not hear.

Facing on the dayhall are the bathrooms . . . foxhole yellow . . . no doors . . . no privacy . . . no toilet paper (PLEASE REQUEST FROM NURSE) . . . and no relief . . . sleeping dorms are locked in the morning and opened up again at bedtime . . . then one can return to one's own little corner . . . restlessness . . . random activity . . . then, the stupor closes in again . . .

Up another flight . . . more of the same . . . Up another flight . . . and the door is open . . . Institutional green changes to bright sunny pastels with vivid posters and pretty murals. Smells of hot coffee and fresh flowers mingle with the sounds of people talking and laughing, a radio reverbrating popular songs and the barking of a friendly Dachshund named Sam. Here are the homey sights and sounds and smells created by the combined talents of diverse Case Aides to make a difference. Thus, the physical house of the program reflected its atmosphere and philosophy as the Case Aides used their imaginations and contacts to obtain paint, furniture, (including refrigerator, stove, T. V., carpeting, etc.) for four offices, three meeting rooms and a kitchen. All of this in what once was a typical ward. The investment and commitment demonstrated by these tangible improvements exclaimed the importance of our clientele. The significance of the surroundings was consistently reiterated to us by our patients, one of whom said, "I always feel so special up here."

THE SPIRIT, THE ATMOSPHERE

A feeling of warmth, concern and purpose pervaded the Case Aide Program, providing a special, somewhat indefinable quality which was its heart. It was this atmosphere which:

- shaped the meaning behind all the techniques, theories, and planning;
- gave the Case Aide a sense of belonging, of being effective, of doing something worthwhile, of making a difference;
- gave the patient a sense of being special, of counting, of being hopeful;
- gave the professionals an appreciation anew of the value of the people-to-people experience and an appreciation also of being part of such positive relationships.

The spirit of the Case Aide program was probably the most important factor in its effectiveness and success with patients. This spirit was so entwined with the total fabric of the program that it can hardly be talked about separately. It is our hope that the feeling will come through in succeeding chapters. All who were involved—the social workers, the patients, and the volunteers—felt that they received much more than they gave, and they gave an awful lot!

GOALS OF THE CASE AIDE PROGRAM

There were four major goals, that the Case Aide program sought to accomplish.

1. The first of these goals was *to help resocialize a mental patient so that he or she may become again a useful citizen capable of making a life with dignity and pride.* "Resocialization" becomes a rather complicated affair in a mental hospital since the "cut-off" patient must overcome a three tiered handi-

cap before he can live again in satisfying relationships with those around him.

The first level of this handicap is undoing the damage of the illness that brought him to the hospital in the first place. He needs to trust again, to be trusted; he needs to accept himself and to be accepted.

The second aspect of resocialization is returning to a world that has been moving, changing, growing, while the patient oftentimes has been standing still, marking time. Mental hospitals, especially state facilities, are populated by "Rip Van Winkles", asleep to the movement and change of the world around them because of their initial illness, the ensuing alienation, and ever increasing isolation as the years go by. Can you imagine the feelings of a person "away" since 1954, 1945, or even 1935, returning to the realities of present day life? The culture shock is enormous, let alone the strain of trying to pick up the pieces of a particular broken life. Children are grown up and like strangers. Spouses are often gone. Friends have disappeared. And, education and skills are hopelessly outmoded.

The third level of the resocialization handicap is perhaps the most devastating. Here, we refer to the effects of living—for a long period of time—in a depersonalizing, bureaucratic institution. This is the antithesis of a self-directed, individualized mode of life—never being allowed to open a door; taking a shower on Wednesday because everyone must do it on that day; wearing hospital-issued clothing, which, while not a uniform, might as well be since everyone else is dressed similarly. To survive in such a system, an individual tends to submerge his own identity replacing it with apathy, conformity to staff expectations, and passivity. As horrible as this may sound and as mind blowing as it might be to the individual experiencing it, soon it becomes the only known, and therefore safe, life style. The simple decisions that we all take for granted are insurmountable obstacles to one who has spent many years institutionalized, e.g. "How will I know when it's time to have lunch?"; or "How much does a bus cost and how do I get it to take me where I want to go?" (provided, of course, that there is enough sense of self left in that person to want to go anywhere).

Many names have been used to describe this phenomenon:

hospitalism, institutionalization, etc. Whatever you might call it, the effects of the process are often more debilitating than the effects of the original psychiatric symptoms. The antidote to such devastating waste of human potential is the time-consuming, patient, and individualized re-education of an "inmate" so that he becomes again a "person". However, with the numbers of such institutionalized patients running into the thousands in many of our hospitals, where do we get the manpower to accomplish this enormous task?

2. The second goal of the Case Aide program was *to provide community residents with an opportunity to learn new skills and to make a meaningful contribution to the life of their community.* The idea behind the Case Aide program was to utilize the vast resources of community residents, on a volunteer basis, to help resocialize mental patients.

The state mental hospital in which we were operating was located in a moderately affluent suburb of a major eastern city. The initial target population sought as volunteers were suburban housewives with under-utilized talents and skills who wanted to make a "real" contribution to their society and who were unsatisfied with the currently available vehicles to do so in their communities. As it grew, the Case Aide population was expanded to include college seniors, graduate students in psychology and social work using the program as practical experience, and career men and women.

The paid professional staff of the program, which was comprised of two social work supervisors, gave the volunteers training in mental health principles and treatment techniques, as well as both individual and group supervision of their work with patients. At the time that we, the paid staff, left the program (see Chapter 6 for full discussion of Program's demise), we were negotiating with local community colleges to legitimize the Case Aide experience as a satellite program for social work paraprofessionals earning degree credits.

It is important to note here that the problems of mental illness have grown to such vast proportions—statistics indicate that 1 out of every 3 hospital beds is now devoted to the mentally ill, not even counting the hordes of troubled people seen in family agencies, psychiatric out-patient clinics, or who just suffer silently—that they cannot possibly be ameliorated by professionals alone for two distinct reasons. Firstly, there just are not enough of us to go around, and even if we were surfeited with psychiatric professionals, it is doubtful that we could afford such an enormous expenditure.

Secondly, it is the growing anomie of our lives that contributes to the alarmingly accelerating incidences of mental illness. What is needed is people-to-people contact, especially to prevent actual breakdowns, hospitalizations, and readmissions. The equality and sharing of the peer relationship, friend to friend, neighbor to neighbor, is desperately needed. In order to attempt such contacts, it is essential that we have a lay population informed about and participating in the alleviation of the mental health problems of their communities.

3. Consequently, the third goal of the program is *to bridge the gap between the mental health service delivery systems of the state hospital and the communities which they serve.* During the past twenty years, and more specifically during the last ten years, there has been growing dissatisfaction with large isolated institutions as a way of coping with the problems of the mentally ill. There is a trend to close down the large facility and to treat people in their own communities, allowing them to continue all or part of their lives and not forcing them to cut all ties in order to obtain assistance with their difficulties.

However, in many of our states, like the one in which we were working, there is a time gap existing now. While the state hospitals are closing, there is nothing to pick up the slack. There is a dearth of services and living facilities for the institutionalized patients being discharged. Community services are better in the preventive area. Fewer and fewer patients are being admitted for the first time to hospitals, but there is, at present, very little for the patient who has already been damaged by the institutionalizing process.

With reference to present community/patient interaction, two points need mentioning. There is, first of all, fear and panic on the part of community residents about having "those people," odd looking ex-patients, walking their streets; the average person does not know what to do with them or for them. At the same time, the patients returning to the community after so many years of institutional living feel and indeed are "out of it"; they continue to be alienated from the community life surrounding them.

If the Case Aide program accomplished nothing else, during

the 8 years we were involved with it, it did provide approximately 300 Case Aides with an intimate awareness of the problems of the mentally ill because they saw such difficulties first hand and had to deal with them directly. The Case Aides have been made conscious of this population in a dramatic way.

Thus, the Case Aide program was educating citizens to be more informed voters and more helpful neighbors through person to person involvement. Case Aides were matched to patients on a one-to-one basis. It was our feeling that parading citizens through the hospital was degrading to both them and the patients they came to "see" as was the "charity" whereby volunteers doled out cookies and cigarettes. While such programs are well intentioned, and perhaps have some place in the scheme of things, they lacked the essential ingredient of personal involvement, of walking in someone else's shoes for however limited a time.

4. The final goal of the Case Aide program was *to extend the treatment reach of the social worker through the use of competent paraprofessionals.* State hospitals are chronically understaffed, overpopulated, and poorly financed. One social worker can realistically give quality service to about 25 patients and their families, a mere drop in the bucket when your population is measured in hundreds or even thousands. The common "solution" of increasing the staff's caseloads accomplishes nothing, since either the same limited number can receive good service or else everyone gets a little, which is a shoddy way to do business when you're dealing with human lives.

We tried to pyramid the knowledge and experience of the social worker who related realistically and intensively to about 25 patients and their families. This meant that the social worker had about 25 hours available per week for patient treatment:

1 social worker 25 hrs. of patient treatment	ratio: 1:25

We built a larger pyramid by supervising and training volunteer paraprofessionals; therefore, we greatly extended the number of patient/families that we could help without appreciably increasing salary cost, professional time invested, and without decreasing the quality or quantity of services. For every hour that we invested in Case Aide supervision, we received from them three hours in face to face contact with patients and their families. (This outline is clarified in Chapter 4):

1 social worker
30 Case Aides ratio: 1:90
90 hrs. patient/families

PHILOSOPHY OF THE CASE AIDE PROGRAM

The philosophy of the program was based on some fundamental principles, one of which was the belief that a firm *relationship* with an individual who really cares is the basis for all change. Friendliness, respect for the rights of each individual, attention to the small details that no one else may have time for, consistency, and the recognition of the dignity of each of our patients mark the atmosphere fostered at all times. It was in this milieu that patients began to experience themselves as worthwhile, important men and women.

The job of the Case Aide was *to help, not to treat.* Because he was dealing with the present, rational, and healthy behavior of the patient, the Case Aide's spontaneous emotional response, under supervision, was the motivating and engaging force vis á vis the patient to accomplish immediately whatever would improve the situation. The Case Aide tried to help the patient obtain what he would need in order to accomplish their agreed upon goals. Financial support, new glasses, transportation to and from job, a room, a foster family, more adequate clothing, social skills, or learning to read and write were secured by the Case Aides who pulled together the resources of the hospital, the community, and their own as well as their patients' creative talents.

As previously mentioned, the thinking behind the program was that patients, especially chronic, long-term hospitalized patients, need to be re-oriented to the world outside the hospital grounds, or de-hospitalized. The Case Aide, having no official status in the hospital hierarchy, was described as "fresh air" by the patients and the mutual approach was "can-do", a positive and enthusiastic attitude. Case Aides, while understanding the enormity of the difficulties that their patients were up against, were not there to become overwhelmed and apathetic themselves. As one Case Aide put it, "We didn't know that it couldn't be done, so we did it!"

Unfortunately, observation of several therapeutic settings with many professionals rarely, if ever, reveals the basic principles of psychiatry, psychology, and social work actually put into practice. Too often, the patient is talked about, instead of talked with, he is planned for, rather than assisted to plan; he may be listened to for one hour a week, but he is rarely heard. Such comments may sound self-righteous; however, they are too true. Time and time again, the question; "How did you get here?", will evoke similar responses in hospital patients:

"In a taxi . . ."

"By bus . . ."

"My father brought me because he was going on a trip and I couldn't go . . ."

"I don't remember; it was so long ago . . ."

"I don't remember. I woke up here . . ."

And so on. We professionals seem to be missing the boat. Where is the treatment relationship we hear so much about? Who really cares about this person, as a person, just like you and me? Do we really take "patients" seriously at all?

Case Aides, novices to the psychiatric arena, are not yet jaded; they not only believe in the principles, but, sometimes to our chagrin, actually live up to them. The program, with the Case Aide as its representative, is the patient's *advocate.* Because the person with a problem often loses his credibility in our general society and most especially in the closed atmosphere of a mental hospital, advocacy is not an easy proposition. How can Joe convince anyone that he is really in pain and not having a psychosomatic reaction? Or that Mary is really better off in a rooming house where she can have the dignity of her personal freedom, rather than remaining in the hospital because she is comfortable there? Or, that it is good for Dave to express his anger when he's angry?

Rather than perpetuating a benevolent despotism which is the prevailing governing spirit of the institution, the program enabled patients to choose to participate, one of the few therapeutic programs about which they really had a choice. Within the limits imposed by our own environment, which did not include money, patients paid their way with their Case

Aides and had to contribute of themselves to maintain their involvement.

While *dignity and self-respect* were the foundation of our work with the hospitalized individual, the system and much of the treatment of the mental hospital, in contrast, forces people to abnegate themselves in order to get "help' . A typical example of the internal logic circles prevalent in many hospitals is: "He must be crazy. After all, he's here!" We have seen patients punished—both physically and emotionally—for refusing to give up control over their own lives, for refusing to sacrifice their identity as people.

The insidious underlying assumptions in "mental-hospitalese" are difficult to confront. The Program did not, for the most part, fall into the traps of professionalism and labelling because it was so constantly in touch with Case Aides, lay people who talked straight, not in psychiatric jargon. For example, when does a man or woman become a "Chronic Undifferentiated Schizophrenic" (see Glossary)—a kind of garbage pail diagnosis used at our hospital to cover all contingencies? At many state hospitals, this psychiatric diagnostic reclassification occurs when there are no more beds in the acute wards. Such labels imply that one is hopeless, unresponsive to available treatment (which isn't very much when your ratio is possibly one doctor to every hundred patients), irreversibly, incurably crazy forever after. Labels are often substituted for people's names, as in "a new paranoid was admitted last night" . . . "we talked about the 'chronics' last week. Let's do the 'acutes' now".

PROGRAM COMPONENTS

When we talk about "the Program", what specifically did this entail? We have discussed the context in which it worked, but what did it do and how did it operate? In later chapters the various components of the Program—the patient, the volunteer, the social worker, the hospital, the communities—will be discussed. Here, however, is a picture of these pieces working together.

Some numbers might help to clarify the operation. For example, during the 1972-73 program year, there was an average of 52 Case Aides and 86 patients involved in any one month (see

Case Aide Handbook). The patient figure tended to be much higher—up to 120—in the fall when new patients are accepted. The number would often drop in the summer months—perhaps down as low as 70—when patients would leave the hospital or terminate with the Program. The number of Case Aides varied similarly, but with a smaller differential from month to month.

The basic ingredient of the program was the relationship between the patient and the Case Aide. Everything else—training seminars, recruitment, collaboration with hospital staff—had been developed and organized to enhance this central core. The perimeters of this relationship were delineated into a "contract" spelled out beforehand to all participants during the screening process. Both Case Aides and patients committed themselves to participate in a relationship under the auspices of the program for at least one hour per week for at least one year. These limits could be expanded if both partners agreed and if such an expansion fitted the purpose of their relationship, but the limits could not be lessened unless the patient could not tolerate this intensity.

In the spring of each year, the two social workers (and the Case Aides themselves) began recruiting and screening potential volunteers and patients. For training purposes, all new Case Aides began together, usually in September, when the program year began. Unless there was an emergency need, this time frame was used for patients as well. Doing the screening in this manner enabled us to recruit for specific needs. For example, if we received several patient referrals from a particular community, we could intensify Case Aide recruitment in that particular area. Or, if it was felt that a particularly disturbed adolescent needed to experience a relationship with the "loving mother", it was possible to look for just such a person.

In any program, however, referrals are never always so neatly timed. We did, therefore, have a cadre of Senior Case Aides who could pick up on a situation, at short notice, at any time during the year.

After their acceptance into the Program, patients were matched to volunteers on a one-to-one basis or placed in one of the eight Case Aide led groups, depending on patient need or preferences. The availability of either modality allowed us and the patient a great deal of flexibility, since it was possible to design a specific program of one, or both, methods at any given time.

The actual program experience began for both Case Aide and patient with their first meeting, always an awkward moment since each knew little or nothing about the other until they were introduced. We deliberately withheld information, such as diagnosis or symptomology, from the Case Aide at this early stage. They had to begin to know one another as two human beings, anxious and unsure but immediately sensing the commonality of feeling that they were experiencing. Thus, the best way to avoid stereotyping and playing psychiatric games was to offer no alternative other than relating to each other as people.

New Case Aides, immediately after their first individual patient meetings, joined their training seminar of 10—12 other case aides who had volunteered that year. These groups were organized around particular days of the week. For example, if 12 people expressed interest in volunteering on Tuesday evening, the seminar met at that time. Once the groups were formed, both membership and the meeting time remained constant. We had a seminar on almost every day, one evening group, and one seminar for senior case aides.

The training seminar continued to meet weekly during the year and was the vehicle that the supervisors used for initial orientation, on-going training, and group supervision. In addition, each supervisor had primary responsibility for the continuing individual supervision of one half of the Case Aides in each group. Individual supervision schedules were shared with Case Aides at the first meeting, as well as time sheets, activity report forms, Case Aide manuals, ets.

The early weeks of these various Case Aide/Patient relationships were used to clarify patient goals, be it de-hospitalization, change of medication, greater family contact, or help in finding a job. These goals continued to be evaluated, accomplished, refined, or abandoned as the relationship between the two developed and planning could be made more specific and realistic.

Case Aides, on behalf of their patients, met with hospital staff, community service personnel, and families of patients. They also worked actively to raise the consciousness of their communities about the needs of their patients.

Many of our Case Aides elected to stay more than one year in the program. As their skills developed, they were encouraged to take on several individual patients, or were trained to lead small therapeutic groups of patients, thereby ever increasing our pyramid reach. Many chose to develop ancillary services that came under the case aide umbrella, such as joint religious services for both hospital and community residents, a clothing store, etc.; whereas, others chose to start new programs within their communities, such as spin-off community Case Aide programs, emergency Case Aide services, and socialization groups for ex-patients living in isolated rural areas.

Now for the other half . . . many patients left the hospital following the one year's contract with the case aide. Others needed two differing Case Aides to accomplish this same goal. Some patients, unable to take the big step outside, did experience at least a sense of their own future with goal-oriented planning, such as joining the Sheltered Workshop or reinstituting family contacts.

CHAPTER 2
THE REASON: THE PATIENTS

". . . to help resocialize a mental patient so that he or she may become again a useful citizen capable of making a life with dignity and pride . . ."

PART I

A DAY IN THE LIFE OF PAUL, A PATIENT

The following remarks were expressed during an interview with Barbara, in the summer of 1973, in the Case Aide Program's offices.

"I sleep in a large back room with about twenty other men in metal beds—rusty and peeling. Ten or eleven of the other guys sleep in two side dorms. I didn't get much sleep last night. You know that guy, Joe? Well, he cried all night again. To get into one of those private rooms, you have to be one of the special patients, like Charlie—he sells the coffee—or little Jimmy—the one who's flipped out all the time. There are no tables or chairs in our dorms so there's no place to store things near your bed. Instead, most of us have a locker in a separate locker room, but they all don't have locks and things get stolen. Okay, the routine . . .

At six in the morning, every morning, the attendant yells down the hall, "Get the fuck out of bed".

Then, we head for the toilet. They just put doors on them. There's vomit in the sink. It's been reported, but the janitor doesn't want to clean it up.

I sit around until 6:30 in the dayhall waiting for breakfast. If I wanna, I can shave. There's this barber—he's really a patient—who shaves all of us—twenty five to thirty guys—with the same razor. He doesn't get paid. The nurse says it's "good therapy". Then, he crawls back on the floor and goes to sleep. He doesn't talk.

Some of the guys get their medication before breakfast. I feel sorry for them because a lot of them get nauseous.

At 6:30 on the dot, everyone on our ward lines up and goes to breakfast when the attendant opens the door. We get around fifteen minutes to eat. It's always, "Come on, hurry up". There's juice, cereal, sometimes eggs, or pastry and coffee. There's seldom milk, except with cereal. It's not very much, especially if you're a big guy like me. If you have a friend in the kitchen, you might get seconds.

(Do you have any crackers here?)

Harry went for a job interview this morning. He had to leave early and missed breakfast. They wouldn't let him go eat with the next ward.

At 7:00, you wait around again. Some patients get their meds; others walk around the grounds, or they go to the canteen if they have any money; or maybe buy a cup of coffee on the ward. The attendants sometimes give you a cigarette for helping out.

If I'm not working, I can go into the patient's lounge and sit there. There's nothing to do, though. There are no books, games or music—only a broken record player. I'm allowed to go to O. T. (Occupational Therapy) two times a week for an hour each time. I can make either a hot plate or one of those paper covered bottles. But, I've done those already.

I could smoke a lot, but I don't have any cigarettes. Or maybe take another walk around the grounds if it's nice out.

If I remember that it's Thursday morning, I go over to the Chapel. There's some lady there who gives you a cup of coffee and a cookie.

I used to work in the chapel for the Reverend. But I didn't get paid so I stopped going after a while. I used to help out by feeding old Mrs. Gordon. I liked her. Even though she was so sick, she liked my company. I really miss her since she died.

There's no place to wash your clothes. Even if you use the bathroom sink, you have to watch them dry or someone will snatch them. So I have to use the hospital laundry now. It doesn't matter so much any more. I don't have much. Clothes are given out once a week by a volunteer department, but Mrs. Bloom goes away for the summer and it's closed.

I wait around until 11:30 and lunch. I hate lunch. Everything looks and tastes the same. I never know if it's fish or chicken croquettes. Sometimes, there's a sign so we'll know.

After lunch—at a quarter to twelve—I wait around. I sit around or take a walk. If I save my dimes all week and buy a big chocolate bar, there's a lady who'll meet you in the hospital tunnel and let you do it with her. I can't do that so much any more. Maybe it's the meds, or because it's so lousy that way. You know, I don't even feel so bad about it any more . . . besides . . . well . . . anyway, it's getting easier the other way—there's this guy in the next bed. At least, it's not for money.

You might earn another dime by going over to the Ad building for the nurse to cash a requisition for a patient who's on restriction.

Sometimes, I wish I could talk to somebody. I can hear the nurses and attendants sitting in their office laughing. The door is closed. On bad days, I think they're laughing at all of us. Last night, there was this party they had. They had some booze and grass. They sounded like they were having a ball. I wished I could go in.

They lock the outside doors at suppertime—4:30. If you have the money, and if you have permission, and you can find someone to unlock the doors, you walk up to Maria's Sub Shop. Curfew is 8 p.m. I have to be back by then or the police will come after me.

Once a week is shower day. It's pretty bad for us guys because there is no privacy even though it feels good to be clean. But it's not nice for the women. They feel lousy with all the young guys—the attendants—watching them.

Once a week, we have a ward meeting for an hour. All forty

of us sit around with the nurse. We're supposed to tell her what's on our minds. But, no one says much.

The new doctors (psychiatric residents) came last week. Like usual, we're all in a group again. It won't last. Pretty soon, they'll be too busy just like the others.

What time is it? Oh, it's late. I guess I better get back to the hospital now."

(Please note that Paul did not view the Case Aide unit as part of the hospital, although he was actually sitting just one floor above his own ward.)

PART II

ON PATIENT-HOOD

The boredom, emptiness, apathy, and bleakness of institutional life is only partially expressed by the man we call "Paul" who dictated these words feeling a little proud, yet pretty self-conscious. He wanted to share his experiences with other people in the vague hope of helping someone else avoid hospitalization or, at least, prepare for it. Yet, he did not really see himself as worth "saving," but rather as hopeless and helpless, doomed to spend the rest of his life in hospitals, though he was only 28 years old at the writing of this book. Because 12 years of his young life were lived in three different state hospitals, his hospital records numbered more than 1000 pages, and most of the information was repetitious and inaccurate.

There seems to be a compulsion among psychiatric caretakers to repeat everyone else's diagnosis before adding their own judgment, which usually only serves to validate and compound what has gone before. An interesting thing happened with Paul; because some doctor or social worker changed the wording of his illness, he went from a diagnosis of "adolescent adjustment hysteria" to "chronic undifferentiated schizophrenia".

At 16, Paul had been sent to a mental hospital because his mother was shocked and upset about his homosexual involvement with another 16 year old boy. Although it is difficult to unravel the real person beneath the years of hospitalization, rejection by his family, medications, and self-hatred, Paul's relationships with case aides and with patients revealed glimmers of natural intelligence, humor, concern for others and other signs of potential health and strength. However, he was most unfortunate to have a family who only visited him irregularly and who were incredibly cruel and disruptive on these rare occasions. They made him promises that they didn't keep and, in general, treated him as a "crazy", "shameful" child. Because his long hospitalizations offered only large quantities of dulling drugs with no opportunity for "talk treatment", he had neither expressed his pain or anger or love nor had he learned appropriate channels for these feelings in a mental hospital. Instead, he learned to submit or to get angry with himself and to hurt himself, because it was more acceptable than yelling at or hitting the offending person. He also saw his homosexuality as a terrible and incurable disease, not recognizing that he had had little opportunity for any other kind of relationship or that homosexuals can lead happy, healthy and productive lives outside of hospital walls.

"Paul" is one person in an institution; there were nearly 1500 people in this particular one when the Case Aide Program began. Over the eight years of the Program's "life", the population was reduced to less than 800. There were several factors—death, shorter hospitalizations, other alternatives, such as nursing homes, case aide work, other staff work, medication, and combinations of some or all of these factors—that were responsible.

What is it to be a "patient"? One can feel the emptiness and loneliness and hopelessness and degradation of Paul. Yet, there is more to "Patienthood". There are "locked doors". Employees have keys—fat bunches of noisy, clinky keys, usually tied about waists or in pockets or pocketbooks. A "patient/person" stands and waits to be let in to his ward, to be let out; to get into the cafeteria, to get out; to go from one building to another; to go to the bathroom; to go to bed. The locking and unlocking ritual confronted us every working day; Case Aides often borrowed our two sets of keys in order to be freer to come and go with their clients. Most of them felt as uncomfortable as we did as they stood fumbling at a doorway with the "patient—person" standing respectfully, subserviently behind, waiting. One woman came up with a simple and beautiful solution; she asked her "friend" (her patient), a young man, to open the door for her and to be responsible for the keys while they were together. It was "therapeutic" in several ways; he felt trusted and responsible, and it was also a socially positive and appropriate response which made him feel gallant. (If this last statement sounds chauvanistic, please appreciate the fact that most of the people in the hospital were quite old-fashioned. They had lived in an unstimulating and unchanging environment and thus maintained whatever ideas and values they had brought with them 5, 10, 15, 25 years before).

One bleak October day, we were sitting in the large cheerful meeting room, (formerly a patients' dormitory that had been lined with 40 rusted metal beds), conducting a patient-case aide group. There were seven men and women from various hospital wards; they were all between the ages of 20 and 30 and all were involved in work training programs. The two college student/case aides and ourselves were meeting with them on a weekly basis to talk about jobs, leaving the hospital, places to live, their hopes, their fears, and their concerns. It was 5:00 p.m. on this particular day and already it was becoming dark outside and the wind was seeping through the barred windows. Suddenly, David, a patient, turned to us and said: "In a few minutes, you'll walk down the stairs, unlock a few doors and leave us and this place behind. Soon, you'll be going to your bright warm house—without barred windows and locked doors. Free to eat, sleep, come and go . . . in charge of your own life. We'll be here with the darkness, bleakness, the wind, the barred windows and locked doors." We "outsiders" sat stunned, realizing how this knowledge—free to come, free to leave—made it possible for us to be in this place. We also felt a flash of shame to be so relieved that soon we would be leaving this depressing atmosphere and going home for the night. Not one of us will ever forget the drama and emotional impact of that moment.

That afternoon group met for a year and became very close to one another. We saw five of the patients leave the hospital for jobs and apartments and two others striving towards similar goals. Yet, that one "dark" moment brought us closer together in feeling what it was like to be a person in an institution. It also motivated us to develop two evening groups the next year, so that the light and warmth of the "outside" could brighten up the monotony of institutional nights.

It is not only the locked doors and barred windows that make "patients" out of people. Large sleeping dormitories of "wall-to-wall" beds give people no way of undressing alone, sleeping unwatched, or keeping clothing or other personal possessions in a suitable place. The lockers for these items are in another room and generally, the locks don't work, causing one's belongings to perpetually "disappear". The petty thievery in an institution creates a terrible tension and fear. Often, it is not one patient stealing from another, but an employee removing valuable objects, (salable items), realizing that no one will believe a patient even if he does know whom to accuse.

This inability to hold on to personal possessions accounts for the large number of institutionalized people who wear institutional clothing rather than taking a chance on losing their own. Also, it fosters a lack of trust and a legitimate suspicion which is not an irrational paranoia. Consequently, what might seem like bizarre behavior is often explicable in this context. For example, "Baggage Bertha" was the hospital joke; when we attended staff meetings, someone usually mentioned her. "Hey, Bertha has a new shopping bag, it's so full, she has to lean over sideways". Laughter . . . a little comic relief for a typically boring and frustrating staff planning conference, dominated with discussion of meds: what kind, how much, how little, how often. One day, I asked: "Does Bertha have a locker?" A nurse replied, "No, I don't think so". It then became apparent why Bertha had been forced to carry all her possessions with her, including her one winter coat, shoes, underwear, pajamas, a few books, old letters, toothbrush, etc. No one had ever stopped to think that Bertha was simply trying to protect her few valued possessions; instead they saw her as "eccentric", a text book case of the "hoarder". An embarrassed and conscientious nurse followed up on this "discovery" and obtained a locker and a lock for Bertha. She also noticed that Bertha still walked peculiarly and arranged for a medical examination and X-rays. It seems this woman was also suffering from painful arthritis, which had been aggravated by her toting heavy bags daily.

While visitors to a hospital are usually shocked by the doorless toilets and shower stalls, they often do not know that a patient also must request toilet paper each time he goes to the bathroom. (This rule is predicated on the possibility that a mental patient might stuff the toilet or waste the paper). Unfortunately, there is also no paper towel or other toweling so people are also unable to wash their hands routinely. It is quite ironic that after teaching children in our culture to observe certain amenities: use a toilet, wash your hands, dress in privacy, shower in privacy, we then remove the very "tools" needed to perform such functions.

In a large institution, privacy and individuality are sacrificed to efficiency and expediency. People on Ward A shower on Tuesday and Saturday at 11 a.m.; medications are at 7, 11, 3, and 7; meals are at 7:30, 12, and 5, (groups eat at 15 minute intervals around each of the "eating hours"). So you eat, take a pill, have your shower and go to sleep with no regard to your own needs. If you have a job off the hospital grounds, you very well may miss breakfast and supper and your shower. Sometimes, with a great deal of arranging and a sympathetic nurse or attendant, you might work out an early shower and a roll to take along on the bus to work.

What does this do to the average person who walked in to the hospital confused or depressed? Soon he is on medication which might "clear up" his head but not to the degree that he is considered ready for discharge. He is assigned a bed among 30 others. His one good suit, clean underwear, (shaving stuff and wallet must be left with the ward nurse for "safe-keeping"), and any other items he or his family packed for him must be crowded into a locker. (If he's lucky he'll get a lock). He undresses for bed with 29 other men, all strangers; he goes to brush his teeth and discovers that there is no toothpaste, no cups, towels or doors on the toilets. He is told to ask the attendant, but the attendant isn't anywhere to be seen. He may have been outside all that day raking the hospital lawn—referred to by the hospital staff as "working therapy". (It is, of course, unpaid labor). He sees a shower stall and though it has no curtain decides it would be refreshing and that it would relax him before sleep; he asks a nurse for a towel and she informs him that his shower day is two days hence. Since there is no soap in the bathroom, he can't even "sponge" off.

The next morning, he is awakened at 6:30 a.m. for medication, although he does not take his meds until noon. Everybody must get up and dress to be ready for breakfast. First shift is at 7:00 a.m.

And, so the day goes, and the new "resident" discovers that he is one of a crowd. There is no difference in the quality of life for a female patient who also has no privacy, and, like her male counterpart, finds herself being observed on the toilet and in the shower by employees as well as patients—often male attendants supervise female showers and vice-versa.

One day, Joan, who rarely spoke (she was in a group of women who were planning to move together to a nursing home), answered our question about "What do you think you will like most in a nursing home?" She said, "After thirty years here, I will finally be able to shower all by myself whenever I want or need one". Such a simple and basic act of living.

Depersonalization is also reinforced by the ill-fitting clothes the hospital supplies which, as we have described, most people wear because they are without their own things due to theft, loss or the choice not to even try to keep them. So, the hospital's other volunteer department distributes clothes (usually the result of well-meaning citizen collection drives) which are in poor condition or very out of style. Also, there is no choice of clothing involved; since 10 shirts are delivered to Ward A for 10 men, each takes what is available or goes without. Over the years, one learns to recognize an institutional inmate. He is generally wearing a shirt that gaps around the third button down; it is also creased because it is not wash n'wear and just gets washed and dried in the hospital laundry. The slacks are too short and are held together at the waist with a piece of rope. The shoes are too large and everyone—male and female—wears them because they were donated by a nearby shoe factory.

Eventually, an inmate acquires "The Patient-look," the result of potent medication, a starchy institutional diet, too little physical exercise, and poor hygiene. He or she shuffles and slouches; the stomach protrudes; the body is flaccid and the hand is often clammy; a handshake is generally loose and without vigor. The face is usually smooth, relatively unlined, the eyes rarely meet yours, the mouth is dry from the medication so that the person is constantly licking his lips or making smacking sounds. Although there is a physical basis for much of this "look," there are also the more subtle factors, such as: low self-esteem, (some of which the person may have brought with him to the institution), learned behavior, (new patients "copy" old patients), boredom, apathy, regression, and loss of sexual identity and individualism. Unquestionably, some people find this neutral, controlled atmosphere comfortable; it can be pleasurable to regress and be a child again—told when to eat, sleep, defecate, and how to behave, to do nothing, to have no responsibilities, to be dirty, and to be isolated from normal social and business pressures. As Brian put it so well: "Here, I read all day, eat, and sleep—I get my 3 squares and a roof over my head; I like being a 'professional patient'." Brian, prior to his hospitalization a year before, was a 32 year old single physicist, supporting an aged blind mother. Because his job was in jeopardy due to his company's cut-backs, Brian became depressed and retreated to his bedroom until his mother, tired of nagging and imploring him, called the family doctor who then called the police. Brian has chosen not to get better; he has learned to play the "hospital game". Whenever a staff person suggests that he is looking better and might want to start looking for a job or return home, he stops eating, sits on the floor and refuses to talk or cooperate. So, he is said to be depressed and to have suffered a relapse; he is then given more anti-depressants and a "reprieve".

There are both patients and staff that enjoy the dependency relationship. In fact, the individual who is quiet, cooperative and seeks staff approval is generally well-cared for and the recipient of special privileges—such as small amounts of money, food, one of the two semi-private bedrooms, better clothing, and cigarettes. This person is very much like the "trustee" in a prison system; he often helps the nurse and attendant with their duties, like feeding and bathing other patients or shaving or "barbering". This patient is rarely referred to any special service of the hospital because staff fears losing him, not only for the assistance he may provide but often out of a sincere fondness. Mary had achieved this special status over 30 years of hospitalization; we became aware of her as a result of another patient's comments. We felt that she would be an excellent candidate for a live-in housekeeper job we had heard of because she had the skills, was only 55 years old, and was extremely healthy mentally and physically. Why was she in the hospital? No one remembered and the hospital records were old and vague. Perhaps she had had a "spell" as a young girl; but, now, 30 years later, her family was long gone and her real family and friends were on Ward X. Nurse

Connors had known her for ten years and depended on her to help care for the 25 other ladies on the ward, some of whom were institutionally regressed and child-like. Nurse Connors represented a kind of employee that we met quite often in our years at this hospital. She was single, older, her whole life had been devoted to her nursing work and for many years she had been an employee in a state institution. Though the work was hard, there were good employee benefits, a strong nurse's union, a civil service system which meant total job security, and, usually, an entire area of the hospital for her to run pretty much as she liked.

This kind of person was, though well meaning, a "smotherer"; she created total dependency in her patients. She called the female patients "my little girls" and the men, "my little boys". Although she was "nurse" or "Miss Connors" to the patients, they were, "Mary, Joanie, honey or blackie", etc.

When we suggested that "her Mary" was perfectly well and able to leave the hospital and that we would like to work with her towards this goal, she became furious. "You'll frighten her and make her sick again; she'll never be able to manage away from me—away from here; she might get hurt out there". Miss Connors warned Mary about us, but Mary was curious; she had heard about Case Aides from other patients. She liked the idea of going out of the hospital with a Case Aide for coffee or a meal, going to a movie or for a walk. She began to wonder about earning money and buying nice clothes, so she "tried" us, and as the weeks of new experiences went by, Mary began to resent Miss Connors' warnings and demands. As she gained confidence her appearance changed and an attractive middle-aged lady emerged from the sloppy, slouchy female patient. She spoke differently, smiled more and began to think and dream and plan for a life outside of the hospital. Within a year, she had moved into a large suburban home to work as a housekeeper for an elderly but spry couple. Her Case Aide continued to visit her and had the pleasure of seeing Mary continue to blossom; she soon became a friend and companion to her employees and travelled with them on some exotic vacations. Meanwhile Miss Connors, though resigned to this loss, kept gleefully predicting that Mary would never last "out there".

Of course, not all nurses are smothering, controlling people.

Amy Burton, who joined the staff soon after her graduation from nursing school, was a petite, dynamic, and idealistic girl who turned a "disaster ward" into a more cheerful, hopeful place. Whether out of good administrative judgment or sheer vindictiveness, the nursing director had assigned Amy to a ward of very disturbed women. It was notorious for being one of the noisiest, dirtiest, and craziest places in the hospital; we rarely got referrals from this ward or even solicited them. But, Amy challenged us; she referred Carol, a 26 year old girl-child. Behind the butch-cut, (the only hair-do the hospital barber could manage), the dirty, tight dress, and the tattered teddy bear was a rational, normal, possibly retarded human being, according to Amy. We assigned Carol to an attractive, mature, and determined case aide, Eileen, who not only had children of her own but had previously done volunteer work with retarded adolescents.

Fortunately, Eileen was better able than most volunteers, or even ourselves, to tolerate the smell, noise, and chaos of Ward X. Though one of us usually accompanied Eileen (with our keys) to her meetings with Carol, she soon chose to manage on her own. It was upsetting and frightening to walk into a large hallway filled with women lying on the floor, women with their dresses off, some defecating on the floor, some crying and moaning. We tried to help Amy with her efforts to improve things; we donated, via our community fund-raising efforts, money to purchase rocking chairs, adult diapers, bright paint for the walls, pictures, and bedspreads, nicer clothes and a radio. With Amy's nursing skills and her support of other staff, much of this infantile and bizarre behavior abated. People responded to being treated differently and many were able to learn new and more appropriate behavior. A simple behavior modification program, using food, money and cigarettes as a reward for good behavior, also helped to change these former patterns. And, Eileen encouraged other case aides to try and work with some of the less regressed patients on this ward. In our group meetings, we shared our fear and repugnance and our guilt; and later, we could share our health and skill and energy to work towards change with these people.

Meanwhile, it was still a slow, difficult, frustrating and exciting year. Carol first gave up the baby-talk she had affected during her 10 years of hospitalization; then, she gave up her Teddy Bear, except for sleeping. With Amy's help, she learned to wash and set her hair, and pick out appropriate clothes for her visits and excursions with Eileen. Without the closely coordinated work of the ward staff and the Case Aide, Carol could not have grown so much and so quickly. In weeks and months, we were attempting to undo years of institutionalization, years of foster homes, and years of being treated as a crazy person, rather than a frightened, confused, and frustrated girl with mental limitations.

Carol is not unique; there are thousands of people who were mis-diagnosed years ago or hospitalized for ridiculous reasons, such as: truancy from school, sexual promiscuity, disobedience to parents, petty larceny and other small misdemeanors, drunkenness or vagrancy. Of the hundreds of patients whom we met, the majority were not mentally ill when we knew them, nor had they been for a number of years. Many of them were still on the same medication because the staff was afraid to stop lest "symptoms" reappear. Though unnecessary institutionalization occurs less today because of new drugs that "cure" symptoms quickly, new laws that protect the individual from quickie hospitalizations, and the pressure on community agencies to serve people in the community, there still are honest mistakes as well as manipulation by punitive family members, politics, and, of course, some people purposely choosing to "escape" the real world pressures.

Carol was the victim of both mis-diagnosis, (she wasn't crazy, just retarded), and legal manipulations; her parents were dead and her aunt, who was the legal guardian, was using the money from the estate. After a lengthy legal hassle, we helped Carol reclaim the remainder of the funds—still considerable—which then enabled her to pay her way in an excellent community halfway house for retarded adults. She has been "out" for nearly two years and has had her ups and downs. It took time not only for her to learn to get along with other people in a more family-style environment, but also to learn to manage money, job training, a social life, and a generally independent and adult life.

In George's story, other important aspects of institutionalization such as the loss of a patient's credibility, the loss of control over his own life, the fallibility of psychiatric diagnosis, and the misuse of staff power over the patient are exemplified.

Hospitalized for 10 years when we met him, George was a man of 40 years, small, dark and wiry. He was labeled a Paranoid Schizophrenic because he had tried to hit his elderly father, had complained of blinding pain in his eyes and said he heard strange sounds in his head. After admission to the hospital, his father moved away, and George who was considered "assaultive" was moved to a back ward, given large doses of tranquillizers so that his aggressiveness would be controlled, and was pretty well forgotten.

By complaining that the medicine did not help his headaches and by using a sharp, biting wit to snipe at both staff and patients he did not like, George was generally considered "a pain in the ass" by the staff. In addition, he would not do ward duty, saying, "Why should I? Are you going to pay me?" One day, he walked up to the Case Aide unit, had a cup of coffee and read some of the books in our meeting-room. After that, feeling welcome, he came up regularly and we soon developed a mutually respectful relationship; he would say: "Good morning ladies, how are you?; how's the coffee today?" After a few weeks, he noticed that we did our own cleaning and offered to help us out. He eventually joined 10 other men and women who met for a "discussion group" with two charming Case Aides. He became the most active and most helpful patient member and soon assumed the role of co-leader, which the two female Case Aides found delightful.

George still complained that the medication made him nauseous and sleepy, that his head ached continuously, and that he wished he could get out of this place so he could get some real medical help. We listened and encouraged him to request a thorough medical checkup, including an EEG. Although legally, every patient was supposed to be given a thorough medical check-up annually, it had been several years since he had had more than a cursory examination, including a psychiatric evaluation, which took about an hour, and generally was conducted by a resident. Finally, after months of his nagging and our diplomatic memos, the psychiatrist in charge arranged for a check-up. He repeatedly told us that George was a notorious complainer and manipulator and we were being silly and naive to encourage this behavior. Meanwhile, he increased George's medication. (To help or punish?) He also sent us a memo defining the characteristics of a Paranoid Schizophrenic and underlined those traits which resembled George's.

Results of physical examination: George Jones had a large benign tumor in his head, located behind his eyes. According to the neurologist who examined him, it was a wonder he could both see and walk around with such pain.

The tumor was very likely present when he was admitted to the hospital 10 years before; his symptoms were similar to any individual with a tumor causing pain, pressure, and erratic behavior. George is still in the hospital awaiting surgery, but somehow he feels "better" just knowing he's sick, not crazy, and he also feels and looks better without those large doses of tranquillizers.

The valuable lesson to learn from George is: look behind the "label", listen to the person, respect the individual, trust your own instincts, and always keep an open mind. Another case in point is Molly, also a "complainer," whose sympathetic and persistent Case Aide was the wife of a well-known physician. When she told her husband about Molly's complaints, (called symptoms outside hospital walls), he told her it sounded serious and that she needed a gynecological exam and pap smear immediately. An appointment was finally arranged by the Case Aide herself in order to expedite things; the doctor reported within a week that Molly had an advanced case of cancer of the uterus which had spread to other organs and was inoperable and terminal. Fortunately, Molly did live long enough to leave the institution and go to a nursing home where she received excellent medical care and warm personal attention, making her last months happier and more comfortable.

Another example of a tragic mistake was Joey, who after years in institutions for the retarded and then a mental institution, was referred to us for some "fathering". The staff was genuinely touched by this handsome 17 year old person who seemed to live in a world of his own—unable to talk, uttering strange sounds, smiling inanely. But, always sweet and gentle like a devoted puppy, he loved to be touched, to be given candy and to follow anyone who was kind to him. At the psychiatrist's suggestion, Mr. Douglas, a retired engineer who had grandchildren of his own and was a warm, helpful man, was assigned to Joey and was eager to give his time and love to the strange young boy.

It was Mr. Douglas who kept wondering about Joey's behavior, feeling that there was something else wrong with him not explained by a diagnosis of retardation or autism, because he saw flickers of intelligence indicating the boy's ability to learn. Soon he had developed a simple education program to teach Joey numbers, colors, letters and a way to express himself. He also requested that Joey be given a hearing test, and he was the only one not surprised to learn that Joey was almost totally deaf and had been since birth. Presently, Joey is in a special residential school for the deaf and soon will be moving into a foster home near this school where he will live with a very unusual family; both parents and one of their two children are deaf and they want to give Joey the chance that they have had to live a normal life.

PART III

"GETTING IT TOGETHER". PATIENTS AND CASE AIDES

We haven't really discussed "who" we worked with and "how" we found each other in the complex hospital system. Initially, there were only a few Case Aides (all female) and two part-time supervisors; so, we tended to focus on the large population of "Chronics," an abbreviated form of the psychiatric classification of Undifferentiated Chronic Schizophrenics. Here, with more than 1500 people crammed into two huge brick receptacles, only a couple of dozen staff members and little therapy available other than heavy medication, the greatest unmet needs were concentrated. Thus, their needs, coupled with the hospital's concern about "trusting" volunteers to work with mental patients, focused our attention on this particular population. Most of our early clients were women between 45 and 60 years old who were considered "burned out"—meaning, few or no symptoms of their mental illness were left; therefore they were "harmless" and "safe" for volunteers, expecially "female" volunteers.

Most referrals resulted from an on-going public relations and educational process, which consisted of our attendance at staff meetings, walking around the wards and chatting with patients and staff informally, or self-referrals where a patient would recommend himself or his friends. We also solicited referrals while drinking quantities of a brown substance that the hospital called coffee with nurses, doctors, attendants, and patients. The Case Aides often "picked up" other people as they visited their assigned client because their friendly smile and pleasant "hello" was the best advertisement that any project could have hoped for. Naturally, patients and staff responded to their friendliness, interest, and positive outlook. In addition to these verbal contacts, we also developed referral forms which stated the objectives of the Program and described the person to whom we might be most helpful. These forms were circulated to individual staff members as well as at various staff conferences. Most referrals were actually made by nurses or social workers; the others came from various sources, including the janitors and the switchboard operators.

There were certain criteria used in screening patients in or out of the Program. A patient had to "reach out" in some way—had to choose to participate—even if this reaching out was only in negative form—such as not throwing the Case Aide out the door. Other criteria which were spelled out for the prospective client during the screening process included the following: the patient had to be able to communicate in some form; the psychiatric symptoms had to be within reasonable control; and, the patient had to have a plan, a motivation a desire to *do* something.

We found that if a patient was either unable or unwilling to communicate, or physically hostile or aggressive to himself or to others, the relationship was too frightening or frustrating for Case Aides. Yet, we did occasionally accept a difficult situation, such as that of Arthur, "the silent musician". We were told by a sensitive and caring attendant about an older man who sat on the ward and spoke to no one but moved his hands in a consistent, but seemingly bizarre pattern. Mrs. Ronson, a dynamic and persistent woman, who had been in the program for two years, became curious and asked if she could try visiting him weekly to see if she could break through this "sound barrier". In reading his hospital record, a few interesting facts could be gleaned from the pages of medical and psychiatric details: he had been a cellist in his youth; his father committed suicide because of drastic financial losses while Arthur was a music student studying in Austria; and Arthur had returned to America to find his broken and depressed mother in a private sanitorium. Then, because he had no money to continue his education and his friends had married or moved away while he was in Europe, he tried to find odd jobs to support himself. Eventually, he retreated to his boarding house room after he had been forced to sell his cello to pay the rent; within a year, the police had removed the unkempt and mumbling 28 year old to the state asylum. When we met him, it was nearly forty years later, yet we saw a glimmer of this intelligence and sensitivity. And, he was still remaining faithful to his boyhood talent and dream by by practicing his "cello", not moving his hands aimlessly or crazily, but making bowing motions over a remembered instrument. After weeks and months of sitting and sharing silences, and one-sided conversations, Mrs. Ronson brought in a record-player and played a recording of Dvorak's cello concerto. Arthur smiled and "played" along with the recording; he also spoke out loud the first words anyone at the hospital had ever heard him utter: "Thank-you, can we hear it again?" If not a miracle, this was a real achievement. After that, Arthur's growth and change were much more rapid; his Case Aide did some more detective work in the records and found out that there was a legal guardian in Arthur's life. We traced him to a well-known law firm and confronted him with our attorney, a law student from a nearby legal-aid bureau. The results were that Arthur received a large sum of money from his parents' estate because some urban property had become extremely valuable over the nearly half a century since Arthur's confinement. His guardian had not been totally dishonest; he had invested the money, had used it, and repaid it—but never visited or sent money to Arthur. Happily, Arthur could now afford the best of care; he left the state institution 3 years ago to live in a beautiful country rest home with other wealthy, older people—who, though not mentally ill, were either "eccentric" or physically incapacitated. Arthur bought a cello and began to play again, to attend concerts, and to make friends. Although he remained a quiet man, his shy, gentle humor and love of music had re-emerged after 40 years of dormancy. And Mrs. Ronson has not forgotten her friend whom she visits regularly.

Despite success with Arthur, it is actually very difficult to "discover" or reach the extremely withdrawn patient because the staff tends to forget about him or her. Also, the very hostile and difficult patient is often purposely ignored, and, as a result, not referred for such a "pleasant" service as that of a Case Aide relationship. At other times, we were referred the most difficult cases as a test or punishment by certain hostile staff members. One such case had a surprise ending.

Vaughan was a small, tough and foul-mouthed 23 year old with numerous hospitalizations for assaultive and drunken behavior, petty larceny, and vagrancy in his past. It was hard to understand why he was sent to a mental institution rather than an alcoholism facility or a jail. Somehow, he ended up on a hospital ward with men who were twice his age and with very different problems. He was noisy, angry, disagreeable, demanding, and involved in almost every fracas, secret drinking party, or illicit sexual activity in the hospital. If he wasn't doing it, he was planning it, or instigating it. Moreover, he spit out his meds, and provoked, criticized, and teased other patients. Of course, the ward staff hated and feared him and consequently referred Vaughan to us with the implied message: "If you're so damn smart, let's see you fix this one".

We were hesitant but were attracted to his youth, energy, and indomitable spirit; we recognized his problems as alcohol dependency, a wretched home and family life, and a lot of typical confused adolescent behavior. So, Carolyn Johnson, a mother of three teen-age sons, "took him on" as her client. When he told her to "fuck-off" the first time she tried to visit him on the ward, she responded in kind and then, while his mouth was still hanging open in shock, she suggested they go for a walk and share a picnic-lunch she had brought along.

Carolyn had the maturity, humor, and instinctive understanding that a mixed-up frightened boy needed. She was firm, consistent, calm and kind—qualities that Vaughan had never known in his own parents or friends. Most importantly, she treated him as a young man with a drinking problem, not a "crazy" person, and therefore asked the doctor to reduce the medication. Then, she found a local dentist willing to make a denture for this young man who had long been ashamed of his toothless visage. Although he was still drinking liquor that was being smuggled in and sold by a hospital employee, he began to care more about his appearance and his behavior. A very important medical fact also came to light when we insisted that Vaughan's physical symptoms of headaches and weight loss required a thorough medical check-up. It turned out that there was a medical basis for much of Vaughan's uncontrolled behavior as well as his head-aches, temper tantrums and assaultiveness when drunk—he was an epileptic who could not tolerate even a small amount of liquor nor most medications. Once he was on the appropriate drugs for this illness, his health and attitude improved. He somehow felt more in control once there was a physical problem that could be treated, having always been terribly ashamed of having a "head" problem. Although, realistically, one could say he still had a "head" problem involving emotional and social problems, Vaughan's own self-image improved so much that he could tackle some of these and allow himself to accept help for the first time. He left the hospital within 6 months, against his psychiatrist's advice but to the rest of the staff's relief. His doctor wanted him to remain in the hospital to "work through" his feelings and to "accept" alcoholism as his problem. Vaughan refused, and, with Carolyn's help, found a job training program and a room in a nearby community. Now, he is a supervisor in the small factory where he had started out five years ago and he lives in an apartment with a co-worker. What is most remarkable, however, is that he returns to the hospital each week on Thursday nights to provide a pizza party for some "old friends" on his former ward. He has helped other fellows find a room and a job and still sends Carolyn a Christmas note each year to say "hi" and "thanks".

These two men are examples of the exceptions to our "rules" because, basically, we tried to adhere to some specific requirements and work with those clients with whom we might have the best results. As a a program of so-called "creampuffs", we were, however, very susceptible to flattery, a sad look, a concerned staff person's "favorite", phone calls, letters, etc. In other words, we rarely said "no" to any referral. We generally tried most situations except the very few who were very regressed (example, a person unable to eat by himself or who soiled himself), or too hostile to tolerate this attention without being harmful to or fearful of others. Another factor that influenced our provision of service was not having enough Case Aides to assign, which led us to develop the group work aspect of the program, discussed elsewhere in this book. The flexibility of the program and its staff, plus a built-in evaluation process, enabled us to "try" a plan for a few months, and, if necessary, change it by transfering Case Aides to a new case or switching within the program so as to make a better "match" between a Case Aide and client. All parties were involved in planning and negotiating so that patients were not referred to us without also being invited to "try" it or to reject it. Our routine was to meet and interview separately all "personnel", which meant patients as well as Case Aides, to discuss who we were, explain the objectives of the program, invite them to visit us again, and think if over. We did this to protect everyone. We also asked both the patient and Case Aide to agree to an informal contract of meeting with each other for a year and trying to work towards reasonable goals for the patient so that the arrangement would be a mutual investment based on reciprocal trust and respect. Moreover, the contract was also negotiable; that is, we supervisors, were available to meet with one or both "parties" to hear compliments, complaints, answer questions or just chat.

As Case Aide and patient, Rhonda and Dan were an unusual "couple"; she was a 20 year old senior in college and he was a 45 year old war veteran, alcoholic, and long-term hospital patient. How they got together was one of those matches of expediency—we needed a Case Aide for Dan, who had been referred by his psychiatrist and had been waiting for two months, but neither a male volunteer nor an older female, our original choices, were available. So, when Rhonda joined us in October, a month after the rest of her Case Aide group, we assigned her to Dan. What had impressed us when we first met him was his sense of humor—he always had a joke or wise-crack. Much of this humor was directed at himself, rarely did he turn it on others; instead, he had become the ward "clown". This man, like so many others after World War II, never managed to fit back into civilian life. After six years in the service, he came back to his small town and found things changed. Without a high school diploma, with a nagging leg injury, and with a big drinking habit, he had difficulty finding a job or holding on to one. He became a drifter; and, eventually, after too many fights in too many bars, he ended up in a state hospital. He was not a criminal but an alcoholic who didn't qualify for an expensive drying out program and wasn't "bad" enough for jail. Consequently, he would be admitted, stay a few months, get discharged, get a job, get drunk and be brought back to the state institution. This cycle was repeated for more than twenty years, and even though sometimes he'd even stay out five or six months, he eventually became such a "good" patient that he became an important cog in the hospital system. He developed skills as a handy-man, became known as "Joe-will-fix-it", and thus didn't have to worry about being discharged. He had become "invisible"—just blending into the ward and into the hospital. If it hadn't been for a zealous psychiatric resident, we too would have missed Dan, but Dr. Stantin proceeded to make a referral, and, upon meeting Dan, we felt that we could help him get some further work rehabilitation skills and help him to leave the hospital. As for the Case Aide, Rhonda was a spunky, big girl, unusually mature and self-confident with a sense of humor that turned out to be her greatest tool for working with Dan. He did not take her seriously; he called her "kid," and, in fact, became very concerned about not disappointing her, making comments like: "Listen, I appreciate your wanting to help an old guy out, but it's too late; I haven't any family, I haven't a home—this is it for me . . . go help some young person". He also was worried that not only would she waste her time, but that she would "fail" in the program and get kicked out by us if "her patient" didn't make it. As he grew to like and respect "the kid", he also began to make a little effort to "help her out", and, thus, motivation began; soon, he was participating for himself without knowing it or daring to admit it. One of the most touching moments in the life of this program occurred the day that Rhonda concluded her year contract with Dan. He gave her his most valued possession, the fake leopard-skin vest that he had worn daily for years.

Probably the second most valuable gift Dan gave to Rhonda and to himself, was his move out of the hospital . . . this time for good. With Rhonda's help and advice, Dan applied for veteran's benefits for which he had been eligible for twenty-plus years. He then left the hospital to live in a home for retired and disabled veterans which became the real home he had been looking for. He also found dignity and self-respect. With his new friends, he went places and did things. He even got a part-time job as general handyman in a local grammar school. He still corresponds with "the Kid", who is now a married woman attending graduate school in social work.

Another "odd couple" was Annette and Ronald. She was a chic, well-educated woman looking for a "meaningful" volunteer experience after years of children's clubs and women' groups. He was a middle-aged, gentle bachelor who had been hospitalized for 15 years since his mother's death. When Ronald was not hallucinating, he was a charming and scholarly man; but when he was hallucinating, he became a rigid martinet rocking angrily in his chair and controlled by the loud voices that told him he was "bad" and "crazy". During these times, medications did not seem to reach Ronald and the staff simply watched over him and let him struggle through it. Annette did something no one else had ever done: she sat with him an hour each day for an entire week, just sharing the fear and pain and craziness. She tried to talk to him about what he was hearing, explaining that, though these voices were very real to him she didn't hear them and he didn't have to obey them. Consequently, Ronald seemed to come out of his psychosis more quickly than ever before, and had fewer episodes that year than in the 15 previous years. Not only did Annette's health and vitality help him gain strength but, by talking to someone about books, politics, clothes, and people, he was provided with a real rather than an imaginary world to respond to. Though it took Ronald one more year, another Case Aide after Annette, who had began graduate school, and some new medication, he eventually became more stable, more comfortable, and ready to move into a half-way house in a neighboring community. There, he continued to gain new experience in everyday living, in thinking for himself and in coping with a variety of situations. It was so gratifying for Annette to visit him later in this attractive house, realizing that only a couple of years before he had been juddling in a rocking chair, unable to look at anyone directly, fearful of leaving the hospital grounds, and terrified of being in a car. Now, he was taking buses, going to movies, and eating out each Sunday in a different restaurant.

A more typical "match" was Lana and Virginia. Lana was another mature and intelligent woman who wanted an interesting and challenging volunteer job while her children were still quite young. And Virginia was an attractive 42 year old divorcee who had tried twice to commit suicide and was sent to the state hospital because the private community hospital in her town refused to take responsibility for her.

Despite their physical resemblance and similar taste in clothes, Lana and Virginia couldn't have had more dissimiliar lives. Lana grew up in a loving middle class Jewish home, attended a fine college, married a professional man, had three beautiful, healthy children, and, in short, had an all American good life. On the other hand, Virginia was illegitimate, grew up in a poor, dirty apartment in a small Southern town, left school at 16 to get a factory job in a slightly larger town. She got pregnant and then married at 17 a man who was twice her age but half as intelligent and sensitive. During her twenty-five years of marriage, he drank, lost jobs, beat her up, beat up their two children, and finally, when she was 42, left her for a younger woman. With both children grown and gone, she decided that life was not worth living. When an over-dose of pills didn't work, she cut her wrists and ended up in a locked ward.

But, underneath the years of suffering, self-pity and feelings of worthlessness, there was a small healthy kernel of hope and strength. When we met Virginia casually one day, sitting on a bench in front of one of the buildings, we struck up a conversation. She wanted to know who we were, what we did and how one got referred to this "interesting" program. So, she referred herself, and, thus took the first step towards health by beginning to care about living again. Lana helped her apply to a nurse's training program to which she could commute while still in the hospital and helped her find a good lawyer so that she could sue her ex-husband for back alimony payments.

Virginia unquestionably had a great deal of hidden strength and natural intelligence or she could not have survived and even grown during all her troubled years. Yet, until someone came along to believe in her, this energy and talent was untapped. Now she had a respectable and rewarding career. Virginia still has her ups and downs; it will take years before she will really like herself and trust others—particularly men. But, she has a good job in a large nursing home, has her own apartment, has made friends and is dating. She calls Lana now the then, just to say "hi". When she's really feeling blue, she just stops by the state institution to see some old friends and some staff and reminds herself of how far she has come.

Not everyone could or would respond to this type of program; as with all human beings, some things work better with one than another. For example, Doug was a sad young man who had spent most of his 26 years in hospitals. In spite of numerous attempts to reach him via drugs and shock therapy, he remained tight in his shell of unreality. Our own efforts, in essence, failed; Doug remained very fearful although he did develop one or two relationships over the years with Case Aides. He sincerely believed that someone might hurt or kill him; his "safety" lay in remaining in the hospital where he would be cared for. Everyone was very kind to Doug. His elderly parents visited him monthly, year after year, hoping that someday their "boy" would come home cured.

PART IV

SUMMARY: BEYOND STATISTICS . . . ARE PEOPLE

In this chapter, we have attempted to turn the numbers and classifications into real people and to make more vivid the quality of these "patients" as men and women with strengths and weakness, loves and fears, dreams and thoughts like all of us. The few that we have described are not representative; they are not the "best" or the "worst". They are simply a few of the people we knew and shared experiences with over the years.

What the Case Aides brought to these institutionalized people was their vitality, their faith, their openness and their honesty. They became the bridge between a world of brick and bars to that world which we call "the community". So many of the 412 people we knew in the 8 years of the program's life had been isolated from everyday living for 1-45 years. Some of these men and women had literally not had a visitor, nor left their ward, nor left the hospital grounds, nor ridden in a car nor on public transportation in many, many years. The simplest experiences that we all take for granted were foreign and frightening for them; so, with many, we had to start with the simplest and most concrete of goals . . . a walk, a ride, a cup of coffee in a donut shop, dialing a phone, shopping. And, a very important difference that Case Aides made was that they saw people, not a diagnosis. In essence, they saw what "could be," not "what was."

And, the men and women who were Case Aides gave of their time, love and energy; though they had periods of discouragement, they kept coming back, and their determination inspired us all. The Case Aides also brought to the hospitalized person community resources; they raised money, solicited clothes, apartment, jobs, medical care, etc. And, when the patient made that "step" out of the hospital, the Case Aide was there to talk to, to share fears and joys with, and to provide the "safety line" between the past and the future. Of course, the relationship needed to change as each party continued to grow and change, and there were both Case Aides and patients who had difficulty "letting go". With supervisory help, both soon were able to go on to new experiences and to know different people. Thus, quite often as a result of this mature and healthy relationship—possibly their "first"—chronically institutionalized people were enabled to transfer this trust and love to others.

For example, even after four years, Lillian still visits Martha in a nursing home. They have become good friends and Martha spends holidays with her "adopted family" because her own family is dead or has moved away. It's hard to believe that when they first met, Martha said: "Listen, lady, no hard feelings, but I don't want to leave the hospital". Yet, over a year later, she was happily ensconced in a small charming nursing home near Lillian's own home, and Martha has become an "assistant" to the Home's director.

Then there was Janey, a 23 year old girl who was depressed and suicidal when she was referred to us, and now, 3 years later, she writes to her Case Aide that she is married and has a beautiful son. It's nice to keep in touch, to know that people called "hopeless", "impossible", "crazy", and other more psychiatric words—are now functioning outside of an institution—working, loving, getting sick, getting well . . . just like other people . . . just like us.

Of course, there are many still in hospitals; some were unable to overcome their fears and repair their damaged self-esteem in the year or two that they had the services of a Case Aide. For some it was too late; they had lost the spirit, the courage, the energy, the motivation to leave the familiarity and safety of the hospital. To them, the uncertainty of a private room or the doubtful advantages of a nursing home were outweighed by the predictability of their hospital ward.

As we explained, there were a few who immediately rejected our program, refusing to "try it" because there was an implicit expectation that anyone who had a Case Aide had a good chance of leaving the hospital. Others chose to enjoy the relationship and then very politely terminated it when the subject of a job, apartment, or family car (discussed in Chapter 6) were mentioned. It was extremely frustrating and depressing to see some of the same nice, sane people sitting on the ward doing nothing, year after year, when we knew that if they tried "the outside", they might like it and adapt to it well. So often, some of the cleverest and most adaptable people and those who were most successful at manipulating the hospital system had become too comfortable in the institution to try something else where they might possibly "fail". We quite often said to a person who was "ready" but hesitating, "Give it a try, if you are unhappy or want to come back to the hospital, we'll drive you back immediately". Those first weeks and months were the most critical; we all were "on call" including Case Aide, supervisors and any hospital staff person who might be involved or interested in that particular patient. We visited, called and continued to help plan. It was very similar to transplanting a delicate flower; the conditions must be optimal, the care intense, yet delicate; and, one cannot relax until the roots "take".

So it was with our trio: Hannah, Johnny and Dottie. Hannah, the case aide, was everyone's image of the perfect grandmother; she was tall and ample, with soft white hair in a bun and twinkly brown eyes that always had a smile in them. She was literally picked up by Dottie, a young retarded girl who was 23 years old but acted more like 16. She had spent almost all of her life in institutions since she was orphaned at 3; her "models" for behavior were other retarded people or older women, many of whom had been dulled by years of shock treatment, lobotomies, drugs, or boredom. Fortunately, Dottie was also the pet of Mrs. McBride, a kindly nurse whose own children were grown and who worked part time at the hospital. The other positive ingredient was Johnny, a 21 year old boy who had been admitted to the hospital by his uncle who was his guardian and only living relative. It seems that Johnny had gotten himself involved with a gang that was into drugs, liquor and petty theft. Though Johnny seemed to have been a more passive member of the group, he still hadn't the motivation to look for more than a temporary job. He just drifted along until his last escapade got him picked up by the police in a drug raid, and this time it was jail or a mental hospital. Dottie and Johnny met, in spite of the hospital's practice of discouraging social mixing of males and females. By the time Dottie saw Hannah on the ward visiting another patient, she and Johnny had already become quite attached to each other. So, she asked Hannah to be "their" Case Aide "because they wanted to get out of the hospital" and get married.

And, in less than a year, their dream came true; one mixed-up boy and one slow, sweet girl had received the counseling wisdom of Hannah, in addition to the support and medical advice of a caring nurse which encouraged them to grow into a more mature and loving couple. Johnny applied for a training program in auto mechanics and, when he felt ready, found a tiny apartment for himself and his bride-to-be. When they left the hospital, we were all invited to their small, beautiful wedding in Mrs. McBride's home. It was difficult to believe that Johnny had grown from a belligerent, angry kid to a gentle, loving person who no longer needed drugs. Although he might still "blow up" occasionally, he had learned to control his temper better—to yell, to walk, to hit a punching bag; more importantly, he learned to love and want to care for a sweet, child-like woman named Dottie. She too had grown and now behaved more like a young woman. She also had her hair styled, bought dentures, and wore the pretty clothes that had been purchased for her by her Case Aide and other hospital friends. Though there were those who predicted failure for this couple, most of the staff and patients were genuinely thrilled with this in-hospital romance. And, Hannah, out of her own kindness and generosity stayed in close touch with them for nearly two years; she even helped them through their first crisis—a marital squabble over budgeting. She was supportive when Johnny lost his first job and excited and proud when he found a better one and when Dottie found a part time job babysitting to help lighten financial pressures. There have been other quarrels, other jobs, two apartments and all the normal ups and downs of any young couple. But, they're on their own but not alone anymore; they have made friends their own age, go to movies and will soon buy a car, just like other people. Hannah sees them less and less, and we know that each day, month, year makes them stronger and more able to manage life's pressures.

So it was with about two hundred patients in that institution; some went home to their families, others to rooms and jobs, others to apartments or foster homes. Some received welfare assistance and others a family allowance. If some became sick or frightened and had to return to the hospital, almost all left again and tried again, perhaps because they had gained from their Case Aide relationship a core of self-esteem which enabled them to grow and bend and hope and learn and live.

CHAPTER III
THE VEHICLE: THE CASE AIDES

> ". . . to provide community residents with an opportunity to learn new skills and to make a meaningful contribution to the life of their community . . ."

Any program stands or falls on the quality of the personnel who are called upon to deliver the service and to implement its goals and philosophy. In our project, these people were the Case Aides who were, in general, interested community residents, with little or no professional training in the field of mental health, and who had a sincere desire to be helpful to other human beings. They were also people who were willing to make a commitment of three or more hours a week for one year. They came from many of the local communities that the state hospital served, bringing life experiences and sometimes formal education to the program. They were housewives, retired corporation executives, nurses, secretaries, engineers, teachers, and college students. Many were exploring avenues for their future careers in mental health professions; some were reorganizing their life styles as they approached middle age; others were "keeping their hand in" while raising their families; all were interested in being of service to others.

Who would want to give up so much time to a mental hospital? What are Case Aides like as people? We have often been asked such questions and can only answer by giving portraits of some of the volunteers.

Bill Taylor was a gentle man, young and idealistic whose career choice in business left him largely unfulfilled. He served as a medic in Vietnam after his college years and came out of the turbulent years of the late sixties unsettled and dissatisfied. He would have liked to enter one of the social service fields, but wanted also the financial security to support a wife and family comfortably. The Case Aide Program was part of his compromise with himself. Bill spanned the generation gap with an ear that could hear "the kids", but with one foot firmly planted in the "Establishment". He related excellently to adolescents precisely because he didn't have all the answers and had just begun to formulate his own personal questions. He was at home with feelings, his own and his patients'. What impressed us most about Bill was his acceptance of people; he made few demands but he was always there when he was needed. Bill drove across two states to pick up a patient who had tried, unsuccessfully, to "go home again", who became disoriented, and was taken into protective custody. Rather than allow this frightened man to travel back to the hospital in an ambulance with strange guards, Bill petitioned for and received permission to escort the patient back. Bill and two of his friends used their camper, one that had been used for several trips that the patient had gone on, to pick him up, and so it was a more familiar and comforting experience.

Mabel Prentiss was a motherly woman in her middle forties. Mabel, who had a high school diploma, sometimes felt intimidated by her lack of academic credentials, but she brought to the patients a common sense in facing problems and an uncanny ability to identify with another human being. Like many of the Case Aides, Mabel had an entire repertoire of living skills so essential to our patients. She was persistent, dogged in a sense, perservering in situations where a lesser soul would have long since run for cover, and could see, as well as bring out, the spark of life in patients deemed hopelessly lost by everyone else. Mabel was married to a sales executive who had to travel extensively. Although she loved being a homemaker, as her family's needs for her in this role diminished, she was able to transfer her talents and energies to the patient population bringing to them the same love, understanding and caring that she had brought to her family life.

Jack Bennet came onto the unit floor for his first meeting, rubbing his hands together, saying, "So what do you want me to do, young lady?" His enthusiasm and warmth were so evident that we felt that he could accomplish anything, and do it yesterday. Jack was white haired, about 50, an engineer, happily married with three children beginning to leave home to establish lives of their own. Successful in his career, used to productivity and getting things done, Jack was always irked by the slow-moving, "double-talking" bureaucratic structure of the hospital. When an elderly man, institutionalized for thirty years, was being discharged and needed to travel cross-country to meet his family, he was understandably terrified and was having second thoughts about his courage. Although this man was not Jack's assigned patient, he "cut the crap", as he put it, and took this new found friend on a personally conducted tour of the airport and then out for a beer. This man got on his plane without turning a hair when the time came to leave, and wrote us later that he had thoroughly enjoyed the excitement of the trip—thanks to Jack. On another occasion, Jack was frustrated trying to help a young man and former patient to be re-admitted to the hospital, since they both felt that the young man was in need of (and, of course, had a right to receive) further care. When the staff refused him because his behavior in the past had been "immoral", Jack threatened to call the newspapers and, consequently, his patient was readmitted and is doing well. Jack had an inexhaustible supply of all kinds of free helpful material, like paper clips and calendars. He was a man who called a spade a shovel and immediately set about digging with it.

Susan Freeman, in her early thirties, with a college degree and two small children, had interrupted a career to have a family. The Case Aide Program was a way for her to maintain some ties with the working world and to avoid the cabin fever so prevalent among young, well educated women at home all day. Susan had taught psychology at a small southern college before her husband's job forced them to relocate in the north, and then the children came. She was toying with the idea of switching to a more actively involving aspect of her field, having always been more interested in the hopes and problems of her students than in the subject matter of her lectures. Susan used her Case Aide experience as a career testing opportunity.

Patty Kowalski was married in her teens and immediately started a family. When she was in her mid-thirties, her children were already adolescents. During the years, on a part-time and piece-meal basis, she had continued her schooling, and was well on her way to an undergraduate degree. She was discovering herself as a person, a woman, and possibly, a professional in her own right. Having grown away from her husband of almost two decades, she was going through an awkward period of marital counselling with both partners seriously considering divorce. Patty was experiencing success in her aspirations, but failure in her marriage; she was in transition—emotionally, physically, and educationally. She got a lot out of her Case Aide experience, but she also gave a lot. She enjoyed the training seminars where she had an opportunity to relate to other seeking people; she—like Susan—was career-testing. Her personal upheavals seemed to have freed up here-to-fore unknown supplies of energy. They provided the experience of how painful change can be in a person's life. She was sensitive to the failures and mistakes—big and small—that characterize the lives of us all, but expecially the emotionally sick.

Irene Smythe brought to the Case Aide Program a long and varied experience of volunteer organizations. She had served as a member of the Junior League, a Gray Lady, was the President of her community's Garden Club, and was a board member of the Family Service Association, to cite just a few of her charitable involvements. In her early fifties, Irene stumbled onto the program somewhat by accident. She had seen a television show with the authors and several Case Aides that was a part of our annual recruitment drive, and Irene became interested. Used to the "finer things", she was quite out of her element and overwhelmed by her initial confrontation with the hospital. She was so appalled by the conditions there that, quite frankly, we never thought she'd stick it out. With supervision, as with all of the Case Aides, Irene was able to project this courage and fortitude toward her patients. Always the gracious lady, she treated everyone, including the institutionalized patient, with the same courtesy, warmth, and tact. She made people feel special; and they responded, blooming in their contacts with her. When Irene came face to face with the appalling needs of the patients, she became a tiger on their behalf, organizing everyone in her circle to help—husband, children, friends, associates—and help they did—with money, with time, with clothing, and anything else that Irene could badger out of them.

And last, but never least, was one of our youngest members—Jackie Levine, a 21 year old senior at a nearby University where she was majoring in psychology. She was an honors student and, under University auspices, was receiving field work credits for her work in the program. Jackie's family was from New York City, solidly middle class, and understandably proud of their daughter's academic powers. Jackie was "into" campus politics and Freud, whom she could quote at length and verbatim. Initially, Jackie had not an ounce of common sense, no sense of humor, wanted everything to be relevant, and was so very serious. Then . . . she began to allow real people, emotions, and the ironies and tragedies of institutional life to penetrate her 15 years of academic training . . . and what a beautiful person emerged from the experience!

These brief personal glimpses of eight case aides are only part of the 277 who participated in the program from 1965-1973. About the group in general;

. . . Of the 285 Case Aides on whom we have records, there were approximately 91% women, 9% men. This lopsided ratio was beginning to change in later years as more men were recruited. Evening seminar groups were arranged to accommodate their work schedules.

. . . 78% of them were married; 16% were single; and only a small portion of them were separated, divorced or widowed.

. . . most Case Aides—37% of them—were between the ages of 40 and 49; 17% were in their twenties; 26% were between 30 and 39; 15% were in their fifties, with only 1% over 60.

. . . almost all of the Case Aides had completed high school and the majority of them, or 72%, were college graduates.

Two percent in addition, had obtained graduate degrees.
... 75% of them went on to other programs, further education, or jobs—all in the mental health or related fields—when they left the Case Aide Program.

About their experiences as Case Aides, in particular:

... 33% spent one year in the program, which was the minimum time required; 40% stayed two years, and 17% gave three or more years to it. In other words, 57% of the Case Aides chose to remain in the program beyond the required time. In the eight years of the program's history, the total drop out rate during the first year of their commitment was only 7% (or 21 individuals).

... 65% of the Case Aides had only one patient. During the later years of the program, when we began to build in skill development opportunities beyond the first year that the Case Aide spent with the program, 29% became involved with several patients simultaneously. 10% conducted patient groups. 8% carried both individual patients and a group. (There is some overlapping of Case Aides in these last three percentages.)

... 15% of the Case Aide population was also involved in special projects, under the Case Aide umbrella, in addition to their individual and/or group patient responsibilities.

That these people came to the hospital to volunteer their energies, talents, and selves to help their fellow men was a constant source of inspiration to us. We at least, had some reasons for being there that did not involve altruism. However meagre, we did get paid for it. They didn't.

Why they came is a question that we cannot really answer because there were so many reasons—conscious and unconscious. We always asked people, in our initial interviews, "why?" and we asked the same question as their year in the program concluded. Here are some of the answers:

"I feel a responsibility, moral and religious, to do something for those less fortunate than I."

"I have an aunt who is mentally ill. I feel that I understand these problems."

"I was a nurse's aide before my marriage; I'm not ready to go back to work yet, but I'd like to get back into this field some day."

"I'm going to graduate school in psychology next year and I'd like the experience."

"A friend of mine was a Case Aide two years ago and recommended the program to me."

"I don't really know, but I'd like to try and see if I can help someone else."

"My father is in an institution in another state; I'd like to help someone like him."

"I'm very interested in mental illness and have done other volunteer work."

"I have some time beyond my job and my family and I'd like to do something for someone who needs a helping hand."

And so on and on and on with responses that indicate mainly a desire to help, a certain curiosity, and perhaps a sense of "There but for the grace of God go I, my friend, my family."

In the long run, their reasons for being there did not matter as much as what they accomplished once they were there. Based on an analysis of the time that they spent at the unit, they were involved in *face to face contact* with their patients an average of 3.7 hours per month, a fact which shows that they actually lived up to the terms of their commitment. This investment on their part enabled 50% of the patients to be discharged from the hospital into independent living situations, family care homes or other alternatives.

What did we do to attract their attention to us? How did we get them to volunteer for this particular program? First of all, we used all the resources of the media to which we had access. We wrote letters to the editors of local newspapers, as well as feature articles on items of special interest to the public, such as state-wide Case Aide conferences that we co-sponsored. Another publicity item was the visit to the unit of a company of actors appearing in a play known for its forthright opinions on the care of the mentally ill. We also used the brief public service announcements available on radio and television. We appeared on guest spots and news features on major television and radio networks. For example, in conjunction with the State Employment Rehabilitation staff assigned to the hospital, we organized a panel discussion with patients who had "made it" on the outside which was covered by a T.V. news team. We appreciated their interest in a "success" story which, we felt, went a long way toward changing public attitudes about ex-patients. We also availed ourselves of programming slots on the public broadcasting channels.

Most important, though, in attracting qualified people, was the personal salesmanship of the Case Aides themselves and others who had contact with the program. If a Case Aide had a good experience in the program, he or she usually involved others. Many of the Case Aides were referred to us in this manner. Such solicitation on the part of our volunteers was ideal since this potential volunteer had already participated in a form of self-selection, or informal screening process. They tended to have a reliable and realistic idea of what they could expect, what would be expected of them, and, as a result, they usually made excellent Case Aides.

We found that our own participation in the organizational life of the communities that the hospital served was another way of advertising the program and keeping it responsive. Some of the methods we used included appearing on panel discussions, speaking at church and community groups, and liaison work with mental health associations and agencies.

We also made a special effort to work with organizations that were attempting to raise the social awareness of their memberships, such as community based mental health associations, the League of Women Voters, the National Organization for Women, and local community colleges. Such groups have a natural affinity for programs such as ours, since we could provide opportunities for training and career testing, as well as personal involvement and active participation.

The psychology, sociology, and counselling departments of the colleges in the area were also attracted to the Case Aide program because it could provide undergraduates and graduate schools with a relevant and practical experience in their chosen fields. In the 1972-73 program year, eight colleges and universities had arranged formal placements for their students. For some of these placements, the time commitment had to be limited to the academic rather than the calendar year.

All of our potential applicants were screened in a personal interview with one, or possibly both, of the social work supervisors. We also required character references. One of the most frequently asked questions about the program was, "What did you look for in a potential Case Aide?" We found that our first impressions were usually a significant indicator of an applicant's potential success. Does this person's appearance reflect a positive image about himself? How does he handle the initial few minutes of the interview? We wanted someone who had a fairly positive outlook about himself and others and who would be able to cope with his own anxieties in an open manner. For example, the applicant who walked into the office complaining about the directions given, and making other negative comments was less likely to succeed than the person who came in smiling and, although nervous and somewhat thrown, perhaps, by his first encounter with the inside of a chronic back ward psychiatric facility, was able to say, "I hope I can be helpful."

We found that certain qualities counted a good deal and that Case Aides needed the "three R's"—reality, relationship and resourcefulness. By reality, we mean a large dose of common sense, an ability to maintain perspective and proportion, and a capacity to "see it like it is", while still keeping a sense of humor. When we talk about relationship, we are saying that we expected a Case Aide to care enough to respect the patient's right to grow in his own way and to be friendly without smothering. Resourcefulness encompasses the ability to put it all together—hospital facilities, supervision, community services, and self—on behalf of the patient.

We also found that we made judgments concerning an applicant's motivation for wanting to join the program. There seemed to be, in our experience, three categories of people who did not make effective Case Aides, which we tried to screen out although they might have been fine people in other situations. The first type may be described as the "super-intellectualizer", usually extremely well read in the psychiatric literature and fascinated by the vagaries of the mind. These people were usually too clinical and detached to be able to relate well to a patient. They wanted to meet a "catatonic schizophrenic", not Joe Smith who really didn't have any "interesting hallucinations" but who desperately needed someone to help him cope with a life situation that was too much for him.

A second category that we tried to avoid was "Mrs. Goody-Two-Shoes" who wanted to help "those" people. A Case Aide needed, first and foremost, to identify and empathize with his patient. They needed to see themselves in others and to see others in themselves. Case Aide language had to be "we" and "us", not "those" and "them."

The third category, perhaps the saddest to turn away, were those people who were experiencing emotional difficulties themselves and saw their involvement with patients as a means of getting vicarious therapy for their own personal problems. Our raison d'être was to treat patients. With that, everyone had more than enough to do; we really did not need to take on volunteers who were also in dire need of help.

As mentioned before, the core of the Case Aide Program was the relationship established between the Case Aide and the patient to whom he was assigned. After the inital screening and acceptance of the Case Aide, the supervisors matched the volunteer to a patient who had also been accepted into the program. This matching was a complicated task; the criteria that were used varied from situation to situation. Factors taken into account included the backgrounds of both patient and volunteer, the special interests of each, their personality characteristics, educational levels, and the therapeutic approach that was initially deemed most efficacious for the patient. An important and over-riding aspect of matching was the geographic home of both patient and volunteer. Patients needed a community connection; thus we tried to match from within the same area. Patients needed a Case Aide who knew where their roots were and who could help to re-establish them. Some matches were quite conventional:

> . . . a forty year old male self-employed engineer to a patient in his late 20's with an engineering background, but with extremely low self-esteem and fears about leaving the protection of the hospital.

. . . a middle-aged, attractive divorcee to a woman patient of comparable age who could not adjust to separation from her parents, who never married, denied her femininity, and turned for solace to alcohol.

. . . a young housewife with three small children living in an isolated suburb to a young housewife, an outpatient, living in almost identical circumstances, but feeling overwhelmed by her family responsibilities.

In these situations, the personal experience of the Case Aide could be brought immediately and specifically to bear. The feeling, "I've been there; I know", was an invaluable foundation for their relationships. These Case Aides needed, in their supervisory meetings, to be helped to maintain their balance and perspective as the problems they encountered with their patients came close to home. The line between the sane and the insane is awfully thin. Additional stress—the proverbial straw—might break anyone's emotional back. The knowledge that this person "made it" gave the patients hope—a tremendous advantage—as they fought their way towards a more satisfying life.

In other situations, we tried different combinations with sometimes dramatic results:

. . . a female college student with an exceptionally mature and accepting manner to an older man without family who was unable to find a place in the world after fighting in World War II, and was therefore restless, and with a long history of negativism, hopelessness, and alcoholism.

. . . a college student named Lisa, who looked much younger than her 21 years, to a woman, Mrs. Johnson, with a twenty-year history of severe marital difficulties and an inability to relate successfully to her five children.

These situations were unconventional in that lay people—Case Aides—became directly involved in the psychiatric difficulty. The Case Aide represented an area of the patient's life—still problematic, unresolved, and coped with unsuccessfully. In the first situation mentioned, the older patient had never resolved early adolescent conflicts surrounding his relationship with women. In the second, the young Case Aide was symbolic of the patient's children who had become all wrapped up in the marital mess. As the relationship between the patient and the Case Aide developed, in a healthy manner, with supervisory assistance, there were immediate improvements in other areas of the patient's life. The important factor that made the difference in these relationships was the emotional courage of the Case Aides: their ability to recognize and accept their feelings—no matter what they were—and those of their patients. At times, this honesty and spontaneity made us flinch, as we did when Lisa related to the seminar group a conversation that she had had with Mrs. Johnson over the weekend. Mrs. Johnson's daughter had telephoned the hospital, inviting mother to lunch in town—an unusual gesture from a girl previously withdrawn and rejected by a sick mother. Mrs. Johnson was unable to cope with her daughter's overture and refused the invitation; however, it disturbed her enough to discuss the incident with Lisa when the pair met later that day. Lisa instinctively blurted out, "That's terrible! You call her right back and accept her invitation! If you don't, I'll drag you there myself!" As social workers, we might have recommended the same action, but would have been more delicate and "professional" about how we expressed it. However, it worked; Mrs. Johnson had a marvelous time, and the luncheon was the beginning of a mother-daughter rapport.

Once Case Aides came into the program, why did they stay? Each had his personal reasons, but we tried to build into the program components that we hoped would enable them to stay should they desire to do so.

As a practical consideration, for continuity and quality of service to patients, Case Aides had to make a commitment which gave them a sense of purpose. The terms of this contract were spelled out during the screening process and was an important factor in our combined decision—*for us* to accept the volunteer; *for the potential Case Aide* to join the Program. This contract, limited and specific, also enabled the Case Aides to volunteer with ease of mind. They could leave with grace. Many volunteer programs ask too much for too long because the terms under which a volunteer offers his services are unclear. The commitment required that the Case Aide must:

1. remain in the Program at least one year,
2. meet with his/her assigned patient once a week, preferably on the same day of each week, for at least one hour;
3. submit weekly written reports on their feelings about these contacts. These reports were the basis for individual supervision including diagnostic evaluation and treatment planning. They were also used in assessing the present and potential skills of the particular volunteer.
4. attend weekly training seminars with other Case Aides.

On the other hand, the Program—or the social work supervisors—had certain obligations to the volunteer. We, in turn, committed ourselves to assist them to do their job. The vehicles that we used were threefold:

1. supervision (further discussed in Chapter 4) of their work with patients on an individual basis and within the context of a group;
2. training seminars;
3. full time availability of the supervisory staff.

These obligations on our part were made specific—individual supervisory conferences were clearly and regularly scheduled; training seminars met weekly for about 90 minutes, and the unit was covered about 45 hours per week.

One of the most important factors that kept Case Aides in the program was their direct work with the patients. Although we tried on several occasions to interest Case Aides in the administrative tasks, such as Senior Case Aides undertaking the individual supervision of the newer volunteers or research projects on Program effectiveness, it was no use. Most of them refused and continued to refuse because they were sustained, exhilarated, and motivated by personal, direct involvement with people. They were making a purposeful contribution and were emotionally connected to their patients and the program.

This emotional connection was so strong that the actual program operations—formal meetings between Case Aides and patients—could not absorb it all. Thus, it spilled over, like capital that could be re-invested—into informal contacts that became part and parcel of the unit's spirit and special-ness. Thus, interest in each other's patients became group outings; wanting to share this experience became evening parties where families of Case Aides and patients got to enjoy each other's company. Or, the desire to assist a patient leaving the hospital after a prolonged stay became a "going-out" luncheon with gifts for the new home.

Instant feedback and recognition played important roles in our success in having Case Aides remain with the program. The volunteers worked hard, often doing unrewarding, dirty, and difficult jobs. They really didn't expect kudos, but we felt that such recognition, from outside the unit, was well deserved and we tried to reinforce the development of relationships with hospital personnel via social get-togethers and conferences. Criticism was, of course, discussed and worked through; however, we often filtered out the defensiveness and hostility of the hospital's bureaucracy about volunteers or about anyone who accomplished anything!

They also stayed for another reason. As the Program grew and developed during its eight years, processing and evaluation made it more sophisticated, therapeutic and professional. As it grew away from its modest beginnings, it became more organized and structured. Thus, the program constantly challenged the Case Aides to develop new skills, to push out the limits of their experience, to try new approaches. We discouraged the volunteers from having the same experience repeated for yet another year. If a Case Aide worked with one patient during the first year, she might work with even two or three or even a group the second year.

In our supervision of these volunteers, we could see clearly the tremendous impact that this program had on them. Their families and friends were enlisted. Husbands or wives, initially doubtful about their spouses spending time at a mental hospital, quickly became a part of the program. They became involved with the program's concern at the waste and the degradation of the hospital population and they identified with its enthusiasm to change this situation.

Having experienced the problems and difficulties of the mentally ill, Case Aides were more informed citizens and, therefore, more thoughtful planners of mental health programs for their communities. Many were able to establish much needed programs through the skills developed while "Case Aide-ing". They could also make more intelligent career choices based on their experiences as volunteers.

Perhaps, however, the most significant impact of the Program was on Case Aides as people. All of them, without exception, were touched and changed by what they were doing. They grew over and above the addition of these new skills and challenging experiences. They learned about themselves, their relationships to others, and their ability to make a difference.

For Ellen Carson, making a difference meant helping a lonely, frail, and elderly woman move into a pleasant nursing home, watching her walk down the hall with her new cane and carrying her brand new suitcase. This was a special and private satisfaction unlike any that she had never known before.

Jean Statler came to the program with years of church volunteer work behind her. Her husband was a minister in a small town and she had always been deeply involved with his work. Yet, she found something new in her Case Aide experience—a personal, individual relationship. She also felt a "freedom"in being Jean Statler—not Mrs. Statler, the minister's wife. Her year in the program was unique; she met other volunteers from a variety of towns and backgrounds and also was the special person in Helen Carter's life. Helen was a 50 year old depressed woman who had been hospitalized since her husband's death a year before. The two women went shopping together or out for lunches and matinees. Soon Helen began dressing and primping for her afternoons out. In less than six months, Jean helped Helen to move to an apartment, and it was difficult to know who was more excited on that happy day. The ladies continued to visit for the full year, and Jean had the gratification of seeing Helen start a part-time job and meeting new friends at a local widow's club.

Sheila Bryan was a quiet, serious young woman who was a Case Aide for four years, including the three years when she was in graduate school. Feeling that her volunteer work was so special, she continued her commitment despite the heavy schedule that graduate school imposed. Presently, she has a full time position as the director of a volunteer program in a community agency.

Ann Carlton had a daytime job, but still found time to share one evening a week. This attractive, single woman found patients on her client's ward so responsive to her that she came an extra evening a week to play her guitar and socialize with them. Soon she had interested a few of her friends in dropping by with her, and thus a spontaneous social club evolved which continued long beyond the Case Aide year.

Harriet Stein was perfectly honest in telling us that her son's recent death was the motivating factor in her joining the program. Her friends told her, "You've got to get involved in something interesting and worthwhile." Her therapist said, "Get out of the house and into a new situation—new people, new challenges." Harriet came to us and said, "Give me a tough case, but not a young man." We assigned her to Linda Stone, a 14 year old girl who had been hospitalized for only a few months and was an angry and outspoken adolescent. Linda heard voices which told her to hurt herself and run away; medication helped her to control her behavior, but her family situation was chaotic. Her mother was an alcoholic, her father a passive man who worked two jobs to make ends meet, and probably also to stay away from an upsetting home. Harriet had to work hard and long to develop a trusting relationship with this sad and volatile girl. Somehow, in spite of the difficulties and the up and down nature of this experience, Harriet felt that she had also gained a great deal. To give and receive trust and love helped her to deal better with her grief and to "move on" in her life. The benefits to Linda were enormous as well; she had found a true friend.

Some of the smallest details and gestures were significant in our work with the institutionalized person: the first time Peggy's patient wore a colorful scarf (like the ones Peggy wore each week) and some lipstick; or the first time that Mary's patient said "thank you" after their hour's visit and car ride; or when stiff, anxious 16-year old Deborah rolled on the grass and laughed out loud.

Anna Smith literally took on the world for her patient, Joanna. The hospital said, "She's too sick." Her husband said, "Don't you dare embarrass me by volunteering in a looney bin!" But Anna said "Yes! She's a lovely person—she deserves a chance; and yes! I will help her in spite of what other people might think". And yes—she did! Joanna left the hospital and, with Anna's determination and realistic planning, found a room and a job. The hospital staff shook their heads with disbelief and a grudging admiration. And Anna's husband met Joanna and began to soften his attitude toward "crazies".

Sometimes Case Aides became overwhelmed and had to stop for awhile. Paula became frightened when her patient, Marilyn, began to call her at home each day and beg her to visit her more than once a week. We helped Paula to say "no" and to set other realistic limits, as well as to deal with her own guilt and anger toward this demanding woman.

We have seen people on the street and in the supermarket who had been in the program 1, 3, or 5 years before, and they say, "It was one of the most difficult things I ever did, but it was also one of the most worthwhile," or, "I'm now a social worker myself and I can't tell you how much I learned from you and from my experience as a Case Aide." Or "My own mother became mentally ill, and although it was terribly difficult and painful, I felt as though I really understood what she was going through and how to be helpful." Or, "You really let us do something; the Case Aide Program was the only program in which the volunteers actually did the 'work' and not the nonsense stuff, like addressing envelopes, making coffee, or just standing around feeling embarrassed".

CHAPTER IV
THE BACKBONE: SUPERVISION

". . . to extend the treatment reach of the social worker through the use of competent paraprofessionals . . ."

The component that brought the various pieces of the Program together was supervision. This interface occurred for two major reasons: supervision was an intrinsic part of our own professional training, and since it was the organizational model with which we were most familiar, we naturally adopted it when dealing with Case Aides.

In addition, we found, as time went on, that this supervisory role brought us into a constant relationship with Program components. It reflected the Program in an immediate and daily way, providing us with instant feedback about what we were doing. So, we kept broadening this arena until we were using this role for a vehicle to accomplish other tasks like training, program planning, evaluation, and consultation.

I. WHAT IS SUPERVISION?

Our own supervisory style has evolved out of our particular experiences and particular professional training. In spite of differences in styles and personalities, we do share a unity of ideas about social work supervision. Most basically, we feel that *it is a practical method of telescoping expertise, experience, and knowledge through various professional levels to the consumer of the service.* Thus, supervision is an integral part of the agency's service, a means to an end, an on-going and dynamic educational process. It is contiguous to agency policies, in-service training, as well as social development programs. These pieces must be intrinsically related to each other in order to have credible supervision.

Let us also say what, in our opinion, supervision is not. Firstly, it is not therapy. Both in social work literature and its practice, there is a great deal of controversy about this aspect of supervision and there are many inconsistencies, both in philosophy and standards.

We brought to our own supervisory experiences a sense of discomfort and dissatisfaction with the practice of supervision as we had known it. We felt that the "supervisor/supervisee" relationship implied a superior/inferior hierarchy which created an artificial barrier to real learning, creative thinking, and independent functioning. There is also disagreement among social work professionals as to whether or not one kind of supervision should be provided for volunteers, another for paraprofessionals, another kind for people with advanced degrees, and perhaps another for students in professional programs. We did not respect this ranking based on such artificial labelling. Rather, recognizing that there are people who are at different levels of education, experience, motivation, ability, and interest, we individualized our response to different needs.

Our guiding principle was that the purpose of supervision was, in the final analysis, to deliver quality service to the patients. To this end, we saw ourselves, the supervisors, as the "enabling partner" of the Case Aide. It was our responsibility to provide him with the tools and the climate in which he could help his patient. And, we tried to implement this ideal in our supervisory contracts. We specified expectations and responsibilities with respect to both partners as clearly as possible—"who does what, when?" Part of the contractual responsibility was a constant evaluation, modification and refinement so that the teaching and learning processes were both viable and concrete.

II. METHODS OF SUPERVISION

In order to avoid a repetition of some of our own unsatisfactory experiences in supervision, we found ourselves both using traditional modalities in flexible combinations and developing new approaches in our work with Case Aides.

The most traditional and formal of the supervisory methods is *individual supervision*. In the Case Aide Program, the initial phase of individual supervision can best be characterized as an exploration and assessment of both Case Aide and patient. There was an initial "getting to know one another" period which lasted a few weeks. During this period, each Case Aide was assigned to one of the two supervisors who was primarily responsible for this person and his caseload.

The first steps in working with new Case Aides were quite concrete and practical, since the anxiety level was usually at its peak. To avoid a build-up of such tension, we had each Case Aide meet his assigned patient immediately, which effectively dispersed the anticipatory anxiety. We also gave them material, such as *The Case Aide Handbook*, individual supervisory conference schedules, and reading material that they could hold onto. In addition, they were immediately introduced to their training seminar where the process of group support was begun with a "How did it go?" meeting.

We started with simple and visible goals such as: "Can we help John to meet you outside the ward instead of in his same "chronic" chair on the ward?" Or, the Case Aide might suggest a walk first, then a trip to a nearby shopping center. As we got to know our supervisees, we began to utilize their own case material in the form of brief weekly written reports. Although they are often a bugaboo in social work, written records of what was happening between patient and Case Aide were necessary, and we planned them carefully to avoid much waste of time with clerical details. After about six weeks, an initial and tentative assessment of the situation was developed in a written form. This procedure was used to assist the Case Aide to evaluate with his patient realistic plans and goals in terms of present functioning.

After this stage, recording was only relevant depending on what was happening in terms of the initial assessment. Suppose the original plan was not working. Why? New facts have changed the situation, perhaps, or our thinking had been quite erroneous. We were always relating to the now, the specific, and to our own activity which could be updated easily. On the other hand, if the plan did work, we were then able to tackle newer and more complex plans. Conferences tended, therefore, to be goal-oriented and practical rather than theoretical and analytic. We also kept in mind that this Case Aide patient relationship would last for one year. Our goals were usually based on time-tables of three month intervals, which allowed us to maintain a ongoing evaluation of our progress.

As the Case Aide and supervisor became even more familiar with each other, the structure and frequency of the conferences became more individualized. We did not believe that the actual time spent in supervision was the important factor, but its quality and relevance. Supervision could occur at lunch, on the elevator, etc. It was the atmosphere of learning, thinking, and discussing that mattered. Some people needed less direction in their weekly planning and could eventually utilize and integrate more complex, theoretical material. Others preferred a more subjective look at themselves and their relationship to their client. Although we did not encourage a "spilling" of personal feelings, the nature of the situation often triggered such out-pourings, and we certainly saw ourselves as responsible professionals as well as compassionate and understanding human beings who would listen. There is a difference between "therapy" and being therapeutic; one of these differences was our ability to set appropriate limits, helping this individual recognize and deal with his or her own problems, and, if necessary, referring this person to an appropriate "helper".

Or, as more importantly and frequently was the case, we began to recognize the Case Aide's and patient's strengths. We tried to organize our work to maximize these advantages rather than spending a great deal of precious time "working through" material that was irrelevant to the task at hand. Why try putting a square peg in a round hole, if, perhaps, you can create a square hole? We could supplement individual relationships with patient groups that were in operation. Or, if Mrs. Jones, a Case Aide, with a particularly mothering manner, was excellent in building trusting relationships with dependent and withdrawn chronic patients, but had difficulty encouraging independent functioning patients, it was possible to switch Case Aides. Mrs. Jones could continue operating with another chronic patient while a more peer-oriented Case Aide was assigned to the original patient.

The termination phase, for both the Case Aide and patient, and the Case Aide and supervisor, was a difficult time. There were two kinds of termination that had to be dealt with; that of the patient and that of the Case Aide. These two usually co-incided, but they might not. The patient may not have been ready at the end of only one year, or he may have been ready before the year was over.

Since the goal of the Program was to de-hospitalize the patient, we used this "year" as the frame of reference in which to accomplish this task. We concentrated our efforts during the last several months on helping both people to work through the separation process. The termination was one of the most difficult and complicated aspects of our Program, as it is in any therapeutic relationship.

For the most part, when the patient was out and beginning a new life, he no longer needed the Case Aide in the same way. The gradual separation was a good thing for the patient who had begun to develop more independent modes of functioning. The Case Aide, having accomplished the assigned tasks was often ready to move on as well.

The Case Aide was asked to write a final summary of patient contact for the hospital and Case Aide Program records. This summary was often the only and/or the most complete personal and social history of the patient, which made it a valuable and relevant task. Simultaneously, the supervisor was also writing an evaluation of the Case Aide, which would be available to that individual and was often useful for future educational or employment applications.

Should the patient not be ready for discharge at the point of the Case Aide's termination, we had to review what alternatives would be most useful to this patient at this time. Do we assign another Case Aide or do we use the information already gleaned to make recommendations to hospital staff about other services that could be utilized? We found it helpful, in those situations, to emphasize the over-all relationship of both Case Aide and patient to the Program, in toto, in the initial contacts. We also achieved such an effect via the availability and back-up of the supervisors. We thought it important to meet each patient and to plan joint interviews periodically; these activities fostered a familiarity with the Program on the part of the patient over and above his relationship with a particular Case Aide. Then, if the termination process was not mutual, the patient still could have a sense of contact with the Program in general, which could support him until a decision was made about re-assignment.

Concurrently with the individual supervision, there was also *group supervision.* Each Case Aide belonged to a Case Aide training group which met weekly for approximately 1½ hours under the co-leadership of the authors. Case Aides were assigned to these groups based on the community in which they (and their patients) lived.

This training group was the vehicle that the supervisors used to impart specific information that the Case Aide needed to know. For example, they had to become familiar with the hospital, its staff, and its structure. In addition, they also needed to begin to know and to relate to one another as well as to the supervisors. And, equally important, it was necessary for the Case Aide to talk about his initial experiences and impressions.

The meetings needed to be most carefully structured during this orientation stage. The Case Aide's anxiety was extremely high and his main support, at this point, came from his sense of commonality with the group. Patient interviewing times, group hours, and conference schedules were firmly maintained. Technical material had proved helpful and reassuring, so we gathered together much of this material into the Case Aide Handbook which was the basis for our initial discussions. It contained topics such as:

Objectives of the Program
Who is the Case Aide?
Responsibilities of the Case Aide—"the Contract"
Some Rules of Thumb: "do's and don'ts"
Relationship
Interviewing
Medication
Classifications of Mental Illness
Steps in Readiness to Leave
Hospital Procedures
Commitment Laws
Hospital Facilities
Readings of Interest
Map of the Hospital

We felt that it was important for all volunteers to have this kind of guide, which was covered in group meetings for the first several weeks. Within this period, there was variation within each training group reflective of the group composition. For example, some groups preferred focusing on the patients, on theories, and on intellectual discussions, while other groups seemed more concerned about relationship. These differences indicated to us the type of techniques that we would use in teaching the individual seminar group. We related to each group where they were. For example, the more "intellectual" groups responded better to formal lectures, reviews of the literature, "professional" guest speakers, and prepared case presentations; whereas the "relators" were more comfortable with movies, low-keyed group and peer supervision, and resource oriented guest speakers.

It was impossible to always have such homogeneous training groups. Yet, our experience has proven that there was usually a dominant faction in the groups, although we certainly respected and tried to respond to the needs of the minority. The training seminar was as already stated, always supplemented by individual supervision.

In the orientation stage, the group was evolving an identity with the Program and with each other. They also became familiar with the facility as they established relationships with their patients. It is important to note that, if the Case Aide had not accomplished all three tasks, but more especially his patient relationship, he would have difficulty persevering in the difficult, demanding, and somewhat unrewarding role as a volunteer in a hospital where he was low man on the professional totem pole.

These groups soon developed into true supervisory seminars. The Case Aides were asked to take more and more responsibility for their own learning as they become more cognizant of the Program's opportunities, their patients' needs and their own goals. They shared more of their own case material with the group, and consequently such group supervision became the vehicle for providing group members with creative new ideas and with tried, successful plans.

Thus, we all moved from the initial stage of establishing a relationship to the gradual use of that relationship on behalf of the patient. This process was expedited within the groups by frequent case presentations and constant evaluation of treatment goals. We also encouraged patient-focused "putting-it-together" sessions, such as, "How can we handle a family who sabotages?", "How do we get John's teeth fixed so he can look for a job comfortably?", "What is a good way to approach Dr. Jones?". The Case Aide has grown beyond a friend/relator to an ombudsman.

As part of this new focus, the supervisors tried to reflect some of the commonality among the diverse patient situations. For example, if one Case Aide group had several patients with problematic family involvements, then we would organize a series of meetings around topics like family dynamics, family therapy, family service resources. Perhaps another area of focus might be community mental health facilities (or lack thereof) including problems of alternative living situations, job opportunities, and after care services. If, to give a very different example, in-hospital situations were the theme, then discussions might concern the hospital's internal power structure and how, if possible, to deal with it, or the integration of the Case Aide into hospital treatment decision.

At the real heart of the training program was this implementation period where the volunteer "made it happen." The supervisors had to maintain a great deal of flexibility in responding to the group needs during this period, as contrasted to the more structured orientation phase. Although we did prepare a monthly plan for each of the different seminar groups, we had to be prepared to dispense with this agenda on short notice. We had to respond immediately to crisis situations and scrap the planned agenda.

During the termination phase, groups served to generalize the experience making it an opportunity for personal growth and an invaluable decompression chambers for emotions like loss, anger, guilt, and relief. The sense of community—one to another—that developed during the year provided each Case Aide with a tremendous amount of support, sustainment, and assistance that contributed to the program's "specialness". The "caring" and "sharing" were so evident that Case Aides' smiles and greetings often met with instant recognition from patients: "Hi, Case Aide. Can I have a Case Aide, too?"

Peer Supervision is a modality that evolved as we matured as a Program. Although we felt that this was an extremely valid and practical technique, it was not as highly valued by Case Aides, especially the newer ones, who were often not secure in nor as appreciative of their special skills and talents as we were. There was still some idealization by many volunteers of the "all-knowing" professional. Peer supervision was fostered among Senior Case Aides and was an important part of their training to lead patient groups. As concerned and motivated paraprofessionals, they could not help but discuss alternatives to what they were doing in order to do it better.

Because of the nature and structure of the Program, we were able to use two techniques—*co-therapy* and *co-supervision*—that proved to be invaluable teaching and learning tools.

In order for people to develop new skills, they need to practice these new activities themselves. What better way to learn than to be able to do? Co-therapy, where both the supervisor and supervisee meet conjointly with a patient, enabled the supervisor to treat, to teach, to learn, to observe, to participate, to evaluate, to demonstrate—all at the same time. This procedure immediately placed the Case Aide in a "partner" relationship where he was responsible, participating, and involved in the supervisory process in a way not otherwise possible. The extremely practical advantages to co-therapy were: the client gained from dual input, it cut down on the time spent in "formal" supervision, and it maximized the contribution of the Case Aide during the early stages of his involvement. Co-therapy also demonstrated the humanness of the supervisor who also made mistakes, hesitated, and made choices that seemed less than satisfactory. This process is the most realistic and honest approach to teaching social work that we have experienced.

Co-supervision evolved from the interest and need of both supervisors to provide support to each other, to learn from one another, and to provide continuity and quality of supervision to all Case Aides. It was also a way of building some accountability and objectivity into a large and dynamic program. One of our major concerns was, "Who supervises the supervisor?" We have some misgivings about the authoritarian quality so prevalent in the practice of supervision and wanted to establish a system of checks and balances. By collaborating with a colleague, the impact of any particular biases we might individually have would be minimized.

By the same token, co-supervision enhanced our supervisory input because each brought a variety of information and skills to the process. We found that, by sharing the leadership in group seminars, we could free up one person to be the observer while the other could be more active. We could also rely on one another's particular expertise simultaneously. For example, when questions about family dynamics came up, Cathy was the "expert"; when questions about hospital or community resources were asked, Barbara was the "expert".

Another use of co-supervision was our joint meeting with a Case Aide when one of us felt that there was not enough progress on a particular case. Also, there were times when one of of us felt uncomfortable with a supervisor/supervisee relationship but could not quite pinpoint the reason. We two might privately discuss our difficulties in working with certain supervisees and thus help each other to overcome them. Or, we might discuss these issues directly with the Case Aide and agree to changing the supervisors.

Such a supervisory team is not more expensive, as might be thought, and is possibly even cheaper than the more commonly used individual system because both supervisors do not have to be always available. A Case Aide could call upon the expertise needed at any particular time and problems can be shifted to the team member available or most able to cope with them.

Heretofore, we have described our use of five modalities of supervision:

1. Individual Supervision
2. Group Supervision
3. Peer Supervision
4. Co-Therapy
5. Co-Supervision

which shared some common characteristics:

a. they were all personalized and reflective of the needs of the individual supervisee;
b. they were all goal oriented;
c. they all sought to educate the individual and to enhance individual's skills and special abilities;
d. they were all based on a "contract" between the Case Aide and the program.

These modalities were similar in their continuity and flexibility.

There were distinct advantages and disadvantages to each of the methods we have described, but unquestionably they all worked best when used in some combination, such as individual and group, or individual and co-supervision, and so on. We did find that there needed to be some individual supervision for all Case Aides, especially in the initial period of involvement, but that it could later be reduced or de-intensified if too much dependency was developing.

By combining these modalities, the supervisors gained new and clearer perspectives and learned from each other and from the different Case Aides. A third and even more important benefit was that the patient got a consensus of planning from these concerned "helpers". And a fourth advantage was that the diverse modes of supervision prevented the growth of unhealthy dependencies on the supervisors and vice versa. However, this diluting process did not mean a lack of personalness, warmth, friendliness, or natural affinity.

Our respect for the Case Aide permeated our philosophy of supervision; it allowed the learning person to take responsibility for his own development. He was expected to make decisions, to develop his own style of relationship, and to participate in evaluating his own work. He was treated as an important and worthwhile person with a right to good supervision; this in turn freed him to give even more to his patient.

III. PROBLEMS IN SUPERVISION

It is important to deal also with the problems that we encountered in supervising the Case Aides. Some of the problems are generalizable to any agency setting, while others are only pertinent to this particular Program. The difficulties fell into four broad categories: personalities, the situation, conflicts in values and philosophy, or the style of the supervisor.

In spite of our screening procedures, we sometimes encountered unforeseeable personality difficulties. Case Aides, once they had become involved with the Program, developed a variety of ways to deal with their confrontation of both the awful conditions of the hospital and the intimacy of the relationship. Some of these coping mechanisms became problematic and had to be dealt with in supervision. The proximity to the emotional and psychological difficulties of the patients triggered, for a few Case Aides, emotional and family problems in their own lives. This category accounted for some Case Aide drop-outs, especially if the Case Aide was unable to recognize what was happening and get to the appropriate help.

Some Case Aides, particularly the younger ones, became overly intellectual in their need to "cut-off" the pain around them. They took to voluminous reading—the more erudite the better—and tended to become overwhelmed by the psychiatric import of what their patients were saying. Or, they became frightened by a sense of responsibility to "do" something—anything—thereby paralyzing themselves with their obsession to define all their activity as the "right" psychiatric technique. They needed help to recognize that a smile might be more therapeutically important than an "interpretation", or, that getting to know Mary as a person, a woman, with wishes, hopes, and dreams would do much more for her than finding the "correct" diagnostic label.

The opposite reaction also occurred. Some Case Aides over-identified with the emotionality of the situation. These volunteers needed help to develop some distance, to temper their somewhat desperate desire to help with rational thought. In these situations, the supervisors had to enforce limits, to encourage careful analysis, and to be ready for emotional crises at any time. A variation on this theme was the person who became hostile and withholding to everyone except his patient, as if he were encouraging a "you and me against the world" conspiracy with his patient. This stereotype had to be uncovered and squelched very early in its development since it was unreal and regressive for both patient and Case Aide. Group supervision usually brought this behavior most clearly and quickly to the surface where it could be handled. Fortunately, we did not have many Case Aides who resorted to this way of coping, since it was so very destructive.

The "Case-Aide-ing" situation seemed to bring out some problems related to the sex of the volunteer. As mentioned in an earlier chapter, most of our volunteers were women. For many of them, the Case Aide Program enabled them to find an outlet, an expression of themselves as worthwhile human beings that they did not seem to have in other aspects of their lives. The ensuing growth of self-confidence, the beginnings of career goals, meant inner changes that were sometimes difficult for their families to understand and accept. For some, old and new conflicts about women and their "place" came into the situation with a vengeance.

To complicate matters even further, both supervisors, as role models, were young, married, with careers, and Barbara, in addition, was the mother of two children. As program directors, aside from having definite opinions about being women ourselves, we were concerned about these conflicts—not so much about *how* they were resolved, but *that* they were resolved—so that the energy being thus diverted could be channeled back to the patients. Therefore, while the Case Aide Program did not pretend to be, or aspire to be, a "consciousness raising" group, we did feel a responsibility to provide a forum for discussion. We found that our own leadership and the support of the rest of the group was extremely helpful to many women in moving forward in their own self development. As is apparent from our statistics, many Case Aides went on to schools and jobs.

Although, over its eight year history, the Case Aide Program was comprised of only 9% men, this figure had grown—to 16% —by 1972. Used to a "time-is-money" way of operating, we generally found that male Case Aides tended to get to the meat of issues more rapidly than their female counterparts and were more interested in results than in the process used to accomplish them. They, in general, wanted to "do" rather than to "learn" and had less of a vested interest in being there than the women. The youth of the two supervisors and the fact that we were both females presented some role conflicts and thinking adjustments for a few. The beginning period of their involvement was difficult for them and for us. Some tended to be embarrassed and uncomfortable in this situation and it took them awhile before they developed confidence in our expertise.

Another, and much more crucial difficulty was the inability of some of them (as with those women who had careers) to tolerate the slow moving and often inane bureaucracy of the institution. Too many head-on confrontations with this red tape craziness tended to create dissidence, anger, defensiveness, and backlash from the hospital which, more often than not, made the patient, not the Case Aide, the scapegoat. We, as supervisors, were in a difficult position: leashing or muzzling the volunteers was unworkable because their perceptions were usually right on the mark and we agreed with them; however, we had to continue to operate within the system, to some degree, in order to protect the patient. Interestingly, male Case Aides were often taken more seriously by the hospital staff simply because they were men.

Variety, as they say, is the spice of life; with the diverse Case Aides in the Program, life sometimes got quite peppery as values and philosophies clashed. We really ran the gamut. On the one hand, there were some people who took our "rules of thumb" so much to heart that they become over-zealous. For example, we strongly emphasized that what happened between the Case Aide and the patient was confidential and that this material would not be shared with family or hospital unless the patient wished it to be or unless there was a clear danger to the patient if such information was withheld, like suicidal threats. Some Case Aides would not even share this information with us—and we had to know. Our judgment, after supervisory discussion, had to prevail in such a situation.

Other Case Aides, either because of too sheltered lives or fanatically religious beliefs, were too naive, which prevented them from recognizing—and accepting—the basic humanity in all of us. A Case Aide like this often encouraged patients to play prolonged games of "Ain't it Awful" or "Why don't you . . . Yes, But" (Erie Berne, MD *Games People Play: The Psychology of Human Relationships*, (Grove Press, New York: 1964) pp. 110-116) accomplishing nothing except keeping the Case Aide on the hook. This type of volunteer was rather sticky to handle because he was too interested in "doing for"; they had to be helped to connect on a more personal level—"Hey, you're putting me on", or "Yes, it is awful, but what are we going to do about it?"

Such conflicts could occur between patient and Case Aide as well as between Case Aide and supervisor. For example, some people everywhere, patients and Case Aides sometimes had difficulty accepting the differences in each other, or these differences became more significant as the treatment needs shifted in the course of the relationship. We had to use the strengths of each Case Aide to accomplish the overall purposes of the Program.

While the authors were remarkably similar in some aspects, we did have totally different personalities and styles of operating which tended to cause conflicts with some of the Case Aides. Cathy is quieter, more intellectual, while Barbara exudes energy and immediacy. Simply because we are what we are, we could drive to distraction some Case Aides assigned to us for individual supervision and vise versa. Luckily, however, opposite numbers were usually complementary, so, with flexibility and honesty, most Case Aides could get the kind of supervision that they needed at any particular time.

IV. ADMINISTRATION IN SUPERVISION

In the Case Aide Program, we were also program directors and were responsible for the over-all administration and management of the Program and its resources—time, limited money, and manpower. In this sense, we were program Supervisors. This role, initially unfamiliar to us as social work practitioners, fit well with our other responsibility of training the Case Aides. One part of our job could grow and develop from the other, constantly responsive one to another.

We developed several tracking systems by which we could evaluate our return on investment ratio. We did this to constantly extend our services as far as possible without sacrificing the quality of those services and to keep those services responsive to the needs of our consumers.

One of these systems was an evaluation of how we all spent our time. What were we doing and how much time was invested in doing it?

USE OF SUPERVISORY TIME—1972-1973 as tabulated for the Handbook:

	Activity	Hours	Percentage
Administrative Tasks	Recording, Research, Evaluation . . .	339	9.0
	Telephone	434	11.5
	Staff Meetings	272	7.2
	Program Planning	731	19.3
	Screening	379	10.0
Supervisory Tasks	Individual Supervision . . .	726	19.3
	Group Supervision . . .	278	7.3
Consultative Tasks	With Hospital Staff . . .	277	7.3
	Community Education . . .	245	6.5
	Special Activities	101	2.7
		3785	100.0

This figure includes hours spent in supervision as well as half of our planning and screening activities. The other activities listed we would have had to invest anyway if we were doing the actual treatment work ourselves.

HOW CASE AIDES SPENT THEIR TIME—1972-1973

	Activity	Hours	Percentage
Administration	Recording	609	10.3
	Planning Staff Meetings	196	3.3
Supervision	Individual	596	9.6
	Group	1195	20.2
Patient Contacts	Patient Interviews . . .	2417	41.0
	Staff Consultation . . .	935	15.6
		5911	100.0

From these tables, it can be seen that the supervisors spent approximately 1,558 hours, or 41.2%, of their time directly involved with Case Aide activities. For this investment, we received a total of 5,911 hours that Case Aides gave to the hospital. This is a return of four hours for every one that the supervisors put in. Not all of these 5,911 hours that Case Aides donated involved work with patients, since they also had administrative responsibilities or supervisory conferences that took them away from their main task. However, for the 1,004 hours, (or the 26.6% of our time) spent directly in actual supervision, we received 3,342 hours (or 56.6% of Case Aide time) in *face to face* interviews with patients or with others directly involved in their patient's care and treatment. This was a ratio of three hours for every one that we gave them. In effect, using the Case Aide system enabled us to quadruple our time input, in general, and to triple our investment in patients.

These ratios were also constantly improving. When the Program first began, for every hour invested in supervision, the Program received only about 1.5 hour return because of its initial reliance on the individual relationship, e.g. each Case Aide had only one patient. For each new patient, a new Case Aide had to be added. When we began encouraging those Case Aides who volunteered for a second year to take on a series of individual patient relationships or a group of patients, we could reach many more who could benefit from our service without increasing our investment or decreasing the quality of the service. As the Program developed a larger and larger cadre of these senior and experienced Case Aides (remember that 57% of the Case Aides stayed longer than the one required year), the extension of the social worker's experience would have become greater and greater.

Thus, you can see the investment in time and manpower to accomplish program goals. What about money? The only money involved was the salaries of the two social workers and their secretary, in addition to supplies, like paper, telephone, electricity, etc. which was a minimal drain when viewed in the perspective of the entire institution which had to be heated and lit anyway. Everything else was FREE; Case Aides were volunteers.

Another aspect of administration, as we saw it, was a constant awareness of issues. We continually searched for commonalities by which we tightened our organizational structure and provided more relevant service. If a number of patients could not realistically plan a life outside the hospital because they had no shoes except bedroom slippers and no warm winter clothing, it was incumbent upon the Program to deal directly with the clothing issue. If a number of Case Aides felt that the civil rights of patients were being violated, it was necessary to obtain legal consultation for the Case Aides and their patients. Such common threads often became outgrowths and offshoots of the Case Aide Program developing into ancillary services like a patients' rights group, a clothing boutique, etc. We tried, as much as possible, to screen problems in and deal with them directly because we felt, quite frankly, that, if we screened them out by limiting what services we provided, they would just continue to fester and grow.

Supervision of the Case Aide Program was one of our most important "tools" in helping the patient to function better and leave the hospital, and it also helped the Case Aide to understand the hierarchy of the hospital in order to manipulate it and to operate within it for the benefit of the patient. Also, the diverse modalities of supervision offered the Case Aide emotional support, skills, and an individual and group identity. We feel that much of the strength of the Program was derived in this manner and also in the structure it provided for all of us—purpose, goals, continuity, and mutual support.

CHAPTER V
PARAPROFESSIONAL GROUP LEADERS[1]

Re-evaluation of Individual Treatment

The traditional modality for the relationship between volunteer and patient in the Case Aide Program had been individual one-to-one meetings. While this mode of contact had been markedly successful in past years, it did present certain drawbacks. The relationship, because of the frequency and the duration of the contact, was necessarily intense. Therefore, patients who did well in the program had to have the ego strength to cope with such a relationship. More withdrawn schizophrenic patients, paranoid personalities, and extremely institutionalized patients were unable to utilize the service; they were "included out" by the nature of the service offered.

Secondly, the termination of this relationship was often quite traumatic for both the patient and the volunteer. Since one of the primary goals of all these relationships was the eventual discharge of the patient back to his community, the termination of the individual relationship often occurred when

[1]Much of the material contained in this chapter has been published separately in the *Journal of Group Psychotherapy*, Vol. 24, Oct. 1974 "Treatment of Long-Term Hospitalized Mental Patients Through the Use of Volunteer as Group Leader"

the supports of the hospital environment were also withdrawn. To prevent the desolation of the patient, these relationships were often extended indefinitely. The dependency needs of the patients were overwhelming in many cases and the very presence of the Case Aides precluded the making of new, healthier, and more independent relationships.

Several external factors also occurred in the spring of 1972 that made us re-evaluate the individual treatment form. Firstly, the demand for the services of the Case Aides throughout the hospital was growing steadily. From 12 volunteers in 1965, the program had grown to include 65 volunteers in 1971. Should this growth continue, the individual supervision of the volunteers would become an impossible task. We wanted to respond to the needs of the hospital without adding additional volunteers, while at the same time maintaining the quality of supervision.

A second factor was the impact of the community mental health movement. Dehospitalization of the chronic patient, as well as briefer stays for the newly admitted patients, were becoming more common goals than in the past. The "back ward" patient was coming to the fore. New modalities had to be developed to work successfully with this population.

In the spring of 1972 we decided to try small groups on a limited scale in an attempt to resolve our own manpower dilemma and to respond to the new type of patient that we were being called upon to help, especially the chronic, "back ward" patient.

Purposes of the Group Project

We knew that a placement in a nursing home was, at this point, the only alternative living situation that could be arranged for many of the extremely institutionalized patients due to the dearth of halfway houses, foster care placements, and state supervised and sponsored apartment dwellings. To be relocated at age 65 in a nursing home, away from a hospital that has been a permanent residence fo 30 years, was a devastating experience. Thus, three purposes became discernable for our group work project:

1. We were hopeful that some patients could learn to socialize before the situation was imminent. If they could relearn the rudiments of social interaction, they could develop social networks that could be transplanted or remade, regardless of where they were living.

2. We also felt that the group might dilute the intensity of the relationship so that more regressed patients might be able to take advantage of the service.

3. We also hypothesized that the group might be a good vehicle to prepare patients for one-to-one relationships.

Training Group Leaders

A. Seminars: As a first step in the establishment of small groups within the Case Aide Unit, we approached volunteers who had been in the program for more than one year, who had shown evidence of skill in a therapeutic relationship, and who were able to use supervision in a sophisticated and constructive manner.

CHART I
PROFILE OF TEAM LEADERS

SEX:	15 female			
AGE:	20-29	30-39	40-49	50-59
	5	3	4	3
MARITAL STATUS:				
Single	Married	Divorced	Widowed	
4	8	2	1	
EDUCATION				
LEVEL:	High School	Bus. College		
	4	1		
Some college	B.A.	Some Grad	M.A.	
5	3	2	1	

FIELDS OF STUDY:

Undergraduate Work: 2 psychology, 2 sociology, 1 art

B.A.: 1 art, 1 history, 1 unknown

Graduate Work: 2 social work

M.A.: 1 sociology

PREVIOUS VOLUNTEER EXPERIENCE:

Little or none	Up to 1 yr.	Over 1 yr.
1	14	13

PLANS FOR CAREER IN MENTAL HEALTH FIELDS:

Yes	No	Undecided
9	5	1

LENGTH OF SERVICE IN CASE AIDE PROGRAM

Range	Average
1-6 yrs.	2.7 yrs.

NUMBER OF ONE-TO-ONE RELATIONSHIPS WITH PATIENT:

Range	Average
1-9	2.3 patients

Thus, a core group of fifteen women was brought together for a training seminar in group process during the summer of 1972. The seminar was conducted by the two social work supervisors within the Unit.

The major requirement for participation in this summer training was that each of the Case Aides involved be willing to become responsible for the organization, screening, and on-going work with an actual group of patients. Meetings were held weekly from the beginning of June through the end of August 1972, and continued thereafter on a bi-monthly basis. The content of the seminar was organized to correspond closely with the specific tasks that the leaders were being called upon to perform.

B. Team Leadership: As a first step within the training seminar, we divided the group into teams of two or three leaders. The team leadership approach was judged most useful for the following reasons:

1. Mutual support and assistance—we felt that the responsibility and the actual work involved would be too overwhelming and time-consuming for a single volunteer.
2. Complementarity of personality and skills—we tried to match team leaders to their strengths. For example a quiet, more intellectual person with a more spirited, "down to earth" one; or a Case Aide with the skill and sense of timing to "tell-it-like-it-is" with a more supportive and motherly volunteer.
3. Check and countercheck—this aspect of multiple group leaders served to handle our own anxiety at beginning a new mode of intervention and to provide us with a multiple viewpoint of what was happening within the various groups.
4. De-intensification and decentralization—In keeping with the philosophy and purposes of the group approach, having team leaders prevented too much dependence by group members on one leader; it also encouraged a sense of group membership in that the leaders shared responsibility and were able to participate in the groups more fully.

C. Content of the Seminars:

Week 1. After designating the various teams, we discussed their anxieties and concerns about working together as well as with a new modality. These feelings were expressed as procedural questions, such as: who do we work with, how, where, who does what, and how often? We delineated together plans of operation. To correspond with the weekly seminars, it was decided that weekly supervisory conferences would be held with each team, each supervisor taking half of the teams. We arranged appropriate negotiating meetings between team leaders and hospital staff to discuss possible patient referrals. All patients referred by staff for this project were interviewed by the Case Aide group leaders. In order to facilitate this screening of patients, we developed guidelines for interviewing potential group members.

The guidelines included the following areas:

1. an introduction and statement of purpose by the Case Aides;
2. a brief get-acquainted period including some information about the patient, such as interests and activities, plans for the future, and their ideas and concerns about their hospitalization;
3. feedback from the patients; their questions about group membership.

It should be noted that all patients joining the program did so *by their choice as well as ours.*

Week 2. By the second seminar meeting, team leaders, for the most part had interviewed prospective group members. The supervisors had reviewed the screening notes. By discussing the idea of a "group contract", the supervisors were able to help the team leaders make decisions about who was appropriate for the group. For example, Mary M., able to work in a sheltered workshop on the hospital grounds, was more comfortably placed with other patients at a similar level of functioning; whereas Joan L., a potential nursing home candidate, would fit in better with more withdrawn and chronic patients.

It was necessary, in this meeting, to reiterate the general philosophy behind the group project: resocialization of chronic patients. Thus, the overall contract for each particular group had to include:

1. group meetings that were held weekly on a consistent basis with the same membership;
2. meetings that were held off the wards, on the Case Aide Unit, where there are gaily painted walls, homey furniture, and where coffee is always hot.
3. Full names were extremely important. Initially, everyone, including team leaders, was given this courtesy.

At this second meeting, to provide additional support, the team leaders were given a bibliography.

Week 3. At this point, team leaders had concluded screening and membership had been determined (clarified later in chart 2). To coincide with the first meeting of the various groups, the third seminar session was devoted to meeting content. We used mimeographed material that had been compiled on the actual meetings of a pilot group held earlier that year.

We formulated certain questions to help the team leaders focus on the following principles of group work:

1. *Contract:* Did the group members and the leaders have the same purpose for being together?

2. *Leadership:* What was the role of the leaders? How did they relate to each other?—to the group?

3. *Group Techniques*: How could seating arrangements, absent members, etc., be utilized to foster group cohesiveness?

Week 4. To validate the group leaders' experiences to date, a well-known group leader was invited to address the seminar. She spoke in a general way about the three basics of any group experience: (1) know your members (patients); (2) have a contract; and (3) try to accomplish the agreed-upon goals. Some of the questions raised by the team leaders included: "Can we really have as a goal helping a patient leave the hospital when we know there are no good alternatives? (the dilemma of the hospital care versus nursing home care)", "How do we handle feelings in the group, both the patient's and our own?", "How does one develop a group feeling among diverse individuals, many of whom are at different levels of functioning?", and "What if a group or a group member isn't working out?"

She was reassuring when she addressed herself to these concerns by stating that even well-trained professionals make mistakes and are concerned with these same problems. She recognized the limited community resources and the particular problems of a state hospital system. And she emphasized the need to be flexible and to re-evaluate the "contract" continuously. We found that such an "outside" validation of what had been occurring for the past few weeks to be a tremendously freeing experience for the somewhat apprehensive group leaders.

From approximately Week 5 and thereafter, the seminar members were a cohesive group themselves, and they utilized the sessions for the sharing and discussion of their actual group experiences.

V. OPERATION OF THE GROUPS

There were eight groups planned and developed. For the sake of clarity and comparison, we have outlined each group in Chart 2. Early in the fall, each group was asked to name itself to encourage a group identity. These names are quite reflective of the group's personality and perception of itself. Three names are particularly distinctive and deserve a more detailed description:

1. "Sam's Early Birds"; they decided to be "early birds" because they wanted to have time for both a group meeting and possible job opportunities. Later, this group adopted a mascot, a fat Daschshund named Sam who belonged to one of the supervisors of the Case Aide Unit. Sam's presence seemed to trigger important feelings and thus was used by the team leaders to encourage verbalization.

2. "The Closet Group": The group originally met in a small room, tucked away in an isolated corner of the Case Aide Unit. The five group members, timid and withdrawn, were particularly impressed with and happy about the lack of bustle and noise so prevalent on their ward. This room quickly came to symbolize, for them, calmness, a more leisurely place in which to think and a place where they could be special.

3. "The Apartment Group": This group derived its name from the goal of the membership, a goal which evolved later in the development of the group. The seven women members, with the help and support of the two leaders, decided to find an apartment for themselves in a nearby community.

A. Content of the Patient/Case Aide Groups: As can be seen in Chart 2, manifested especially in the number of years of hospitalization and the nature of the patient's illnesses, we were dealing with a middle-aged, extremely institutionalized population of chronic patients. The typical group member was often inappropriately dressed, unkempt, apathetic-looking; they tended to shuffle rather than walk; their overall bearing was whipped and hopeless.

The first task of the team leaders was to encourage interaction among the members. The keynote of these initial meetings was the imaginative style of each of our leaders. Their techniques ranged from the simple, like name tags, to the subtle device of tape recordings to validate the patients' sense of "being there". All the team leaders quickly learned the value of serving food (coffee and cake) as both a communal experience and a non-verbal demonstration of hospitality, concern and respect.

Since the goal of the groups was re-socialization, the focus was on the present and future. Discussions pertaining to diagnosis or illnesses were discouraged and rarely came up. The members' social and communicative skills were truly rusty. Most of these patients, for at least twenty years, had had no opportunity to be individuals with likes, desires, or interests. Even in social activities sponsored by the hospital, the parties were organized *for* them as *patients*, not people. These patient/ Case Aide groups were different:

> The Merry Group supported William's difficult struggle to voice one sentence, "I like oysters!" He glowed . . . from a sense of accomplishment. The other members began to applaud because they had heard him; they knew what an important moment this was.
>
> The first time Robert spoke in his group was to describe a poignant moment in his past. This disheveled, toothless 45 year old man gently evoked an image of ice skating alone on a moonlit pond with his girl friend of 25 years ago. Other group members and leaders alike sat silently; their faces reflected his own sadness and loss. Though it was not stated, all appreciated his entrusting to them this special and beautiful memory.

To enhance the interaction, all team leaders helped their members to plan a group activity. Sharing an experience together was an important dimension in the development of group cohesiveness. For example, Sam's Early Birds went bowling, the Social Group made brownies, the Merry Group planned a complete luncheon, the Closet Group went to dinner and a show, the Family Group had a barbecue, the Ivory Tower and Apartment Groups helped a member apartment hunt.

After approximately 10-15 meetings, certain goals had been accomplished. They were *groups*: people were talking to each other, not just to the leaders. Discussions were spontaneous, real, and at times heated, including themes like the elections,

CHART 2

COMPOSITION OF CASE AIDE-LED GROUPS

	The Apartment Group	The Closet Group	The Family Group	The Ivory Tower
Average age:	40 years	58 years	51 years	54 years
Sex:	7F —	5F —	3F 5M	3F 5M
Average Stay in Hospital	9 years	23 years	19 years	16 years
Family Visits:				
Regular	4	1	—	3
Irregular	3	3	3	—
None	—	1	5	3
Diagnosis:	5 Chronic undifferentiated schizophrenic 2 manic depressive	3 Chronic undifferentiated schizophrenic 1 manic depressive 1 mentally deficient	5 Chronic undifferentiated schizophrenic 1 mentally deficient 1 organic brain syndrome 1 alcohol addiction	5 Chronic undifferentiated schizophrenic 1 mentally deficient
Hospital Staff Goals	Placement off ward, relating.	Refer to nursing home at age 65	Placement off ward	Placement off ward

	The Merry Group	Sam's Early Birds	The Social Group	The Sunshine Group
Average Age:	57 years	43 years	53 years	54 years
Sex:	7F 4M	3F 3M	5F 4M	14F —
Average Stay in Hospital:	28 years	19 years	23 years	20 years
Family Visits:				
Regular	2	4	3	5
Irregular	6	1	3	1
None	3	1	3	8
Diagnosis:	10 Chronic undifferentiated schizophrenic 1 mentally deficient	4 Chronic undifferentiated schizophrenic 2 mentally deficient	5 Chronic undifferentiated schizophrenic 4 chronic brain syndrome	11 Chronic undifferentiated Schizophrenic 2 mentally deficient 1 chronic brain syndrome
Hospital Staff Goals:	nursing home—socialization	socialization, job support, group support communication	social experience	placement off ward, social experience, make friends.

literature, music, and the hospital. Appearances were improved by smiling and a sense of alertness; members "dressed up" for meetings. This was the point where the groups named themselves. It was evident to us that the goal of the re-socialization was being accomplished.

B. Change of Contract: After about 12 meetings, the team leaders began both in the seminars and in individual supervision to become uncomfortable and uncertain about changes occurring within the groups. It became obvious from their material that the patients were beginning to use the group meetings in a very different way.

The Social Group, in spite of their name, said it for all groups when they decided that they did not want to do anything or go anywhere. They just wanted to "talk". "To talk" meant:

1. Personal and particular discussions: Dorothy said to Alice, "It's your fault. You don't try to do anything about yourself." George said to Charles, "You're talking too much. Give someone else a chance." And Harold said to the group, "Guess what happened to me today!"

2. More universal feelings: Janice expressed anger and pain at not having been invited to her sister's wedding. Paul said, "Working and making money aren't enough. You need something else. You have to be told by someone you care about that it matters." And Ellen said, "Hey, I'm me!"

To generalize, there were certain themes that evolved in all of the groups, although they were expressed at different times and in different ways. The most prevalent of these was the sense of loneliness, loss, and fear of the future. As can be seen in Chart 2, the majority of the patients had little or no family contact, and they began to express their feelings of pain and anger at this rejection. The realistic side of these feelings is that it is very difficult, almost impossible, to become again an active community person with no one "on the outside" who cares.

C. The Team Leaders' Response: At first, the team leaders questioned their ability to cope with the raw feelings that were coming out. They were afraid of not going far enough, of going too far, of making things worse. As one leader put it, "Is it really fair to allow such heavy discussions in a one-hour week meeting. Then they go back to the ward where there is no one who has the time to listen?"

In the training seminar for the group leaders, we helped them to verbalize and examine their fear of this kind of responsibility and their lack of self-confidence. Again, the close correlation between the content of both the training seminar and the patient/Case Aide group meetings was critical. The leaders were helped to utilize the seminar to discuss their own feelings; this "group" experience freed them. When they understood the value of sharing and support for themselves, they were able to allow, encourage, and handle this material in their groups.

Some of the leaders were more able to grow and accept these changes than others. It was at this point that they needed much more individual supervision, especially when different growth rates occurred between team leaders. We found that we could identify three models:

1. Some team leaders used their differences consciously and in a constructive manner. They maintained a clearer role separation purposefully. For example, one leader might be more supportive or "mothering", while the other could be more interpretive, or "fathering".
2. Some team leaders experienced conflict among themselves and became paralyzed or angry; these leaders needed a great deal of help and basically had to "fight it out".
3. In certain instances, where there were three leaders, two became polarized as above. The third was more neutral and evolved a new role as the mediator.

D. Implementation, or "Putting it Together": The direct result was an enormous opening-up of the whole project; we saw real changes in all the groups. Some of these changes were superficial but valid, such as:

1. Most patients were arriving earlier for group meetings and staying later.
2. Patients initiated their own devices for providing refreshments via bake sales, barter, etc.
3. They were referring other patients to the project.
4. Patients were becoming interested in exploring job opportunities even if they would be starting the job on a volunteer basis.

Out of the 66 group members during the period from 1972-73,

19% were discharged from the hospital during the first year; of these, 6% obtained employment in the community;

20% went to work in the hospital's sheltered workshop for pay;
23% went to work in the hospital without pay;
less than 1% dropped out.

CHAPTER VI
THE STORY:

THE DEVELOPMENT OF THE CASE AIDE PROGRAM

1. Beginnings

The Case Aide Program originated outside the hospital setting. It was founded in 1965 by the representatives of two local mental health associations. The original purpose was to provide community contact for chronically hospitalized mental patients. The first volunteers were recruited from housewives with child-rearing experiences. It was felt that the skills used in coping with growing children were translatable to helping the mentally ill. A funding grant was obtained from an area charitable foundation and was scheduled to last for five years. The mental health association representatives formed themselves into an advisory board for the Program.

The function and structure of this original committee was as follows: It consisted of two members from each of the towns represented by the two mental health associations; then, they (about 20 representatives) elected a board of eight people who actually administered and supervised the program and its staff of two social workers. The first social worker was hired and appointed director. Barbara, who was hired by this board six months later, was the associate director. All publicity, recruiting of Case Aides, and fund raising was done by this group of eight people. The initial relationship between program staff and board was excellent. There was healthy respect and high morale all around. The social workers were allowed to develop the project using their own creativity and professional skills; the board functioned primarily outside of the hospital, doing what they did best—educating other community people, publicizing the program, attracting new volunteers and raising money to expand the project. The social workers met with the board monthly, submitting written reports outlining their activities. After several months, only the Program Director met with the board to avoid duplication of effort; thus Barbara, and later the other part time social workers who joined the staff, were excluded, and only submitted their reports and attended annual luncheons. More about this relationship later.

In 1965, the Case Aide staff consisted of one part-time social worker and twelve volunteers. The structure was influenced by a pilot project at another larger urban state mental facility. The Case Aide Board approached the administration of "our" hospital (which was smaller and suburban), requesting that the service be allowed to operate within its walls. The trade-off for the hospital was obtaining "brownie points" for innovativeness, in addition to free friendly visiting with patients. At this time, the potential therapeutic effect was not really recognized. The agreement to allow the Program admittance also enabled the hospital superintendant to pay lip service to the new community involvement concepts, deflecting the community's attention while isolating the volunteers on chronic back wards. The first volunteers were the traditional young to middle aged females with families to raise and a need to "do" something for less fortunate people. The program was either not taken seriously or was too threatening to hospital personnel from the very beginning. Records were "not available"; staff ignored or were hostile to the interlopers to the degree that some department heads refused to allow their staff to make referrals to, or to cooperate with, the program. The Case Aide Director and Associate Director under the direction of the advisory boards responded by "selling" the program in a low-keyed and relatively non-threatening manner. Such an approach was the only possible way to enable the program to survive initially and to carve a niche for itself in the hospital system. But, as a result of this strategy, the program staff were never really seen as professionals who had a valid service to offer to both patients and staff, but only as volunteer "trainers". All confrontations within the system were avoided at all costs; thus, no mechanics for the program's input or for constructive negotiations were developed.

The Case Aide Program grew during the next three years. New social workers were employed on a part-time and piecemeal basis. No overall administration was designed, nor were programs and procedures unified. Each staff person was responsible for a certain number of volunteers and operated autonomously only reporting jointly to the Case Aide Board. This Board had gradually diminished in membership until only four women remained. These four maintained only a minimal relationship with the original mental health associations who had been instrumental in the program's foundation.

As the programs grew, the original structure and model were just stretched, rather than evaluated or re-vamped according to new needs and situations. The structure could not accommodate three staff members and 45 volunteers all doing their own thing when it had been originally designed to handle one social worker and twelve volunteers.

After three years, this structure had become rigid and somewhat sacrosanct to both the director and the four board members. The original director of the program had developed an extremely close relationship with the board members, and, as mentioned above, she alone had dealt with them. They made all the decisions pertaining to the program, including the hiring and firing of staff.

New hospital populations and more diverse volunteers were ignored. An adjunct to the rigidity of structure was the corresponding rigidity of modality, i.e. the one-to-one relationships. Such an organizational feature meant that, for each new patient accepted into the program, a corresponding "new" volunteer had to be recruited. Thus, eventually, the growth of the program had to be limited because of the excessive demand on the supervisors' time.

The first of several important developments began in 1968

when the director of the program resigned. Barbara then became the acting director and another part-time social worker became her assistant. The next major change happened in 1970 when the original funding grant ran out. This latter crisis became a turning point for the entire program. The Board decided to seek public funding from the state department of mental health which was also responsible for the financing of all state mental health facilities. The Board, in effect, went over the hospital superintendent's head by dealing with his superiors in the department and with local politicians. And, not having confidence in the new acting director and her assistant, they also left them out of their negotiations. To sweeten the deal for the hospital superintendent, the Board offered to lobby for the superintendent's pet project in return for the Case Aide Program's receiving top priority in his proposed budget. When the program was approved, it was assigned to the hospital. Thus, the dictum for the Case Aide service came from above and was superimposed on a reluctant hospital system.

The negotiations were done primarily by the Case Aide board which was composed of this quartet of well-intentioned, but somewhat naive lay people. They had not allowed new membership on the board and were accustomed to total autonomy. In their eagerness to be funded and to survive financially, they overrode professional and practical issues.

They obtained two equal social work supervisory positions in addition to one secretarial position. The two social workers in the program were called co-directors receiving equal pay and having equal responsibility. Unfortunately, they had unequal professional backgrounds and conflicting philosophies. Internally, such a move proved disastrous. There were no clear lines of authority, responsibility, or decision making, and very soon overt conflict and competition developed. The Case Aide board remained more than an advisory group as a result of this conflict and they assumed more of the administrative responsibility without having a clear idea of what they were administering, since they were not knowledgeable in social work practice or supervision. For example, to accomplish a task, the two social workers would have to consult with the board. Since none of the participants understood who was in charge and decisions had to evolve via group process, which often proved time-consuming and inefficient, the program just stagnated. There was no mechanism for program evaluation or long-term planning and no organized statistical data on which to predicate growth and development. Furthermore, there was an uneven quality to the program which was running in two different directions with two different leaders.

At the time of these negotiations with the hospital, the program was put structurally in the social service department without the full participation of that department's director. The accommodation to the program's arrival was made with as little effort as possible—it was housed as far away as physically possible from other staff persons and on the same back wards as the most forgotten patients. The grafting on of the program to the rest of the hospital as an afterthought really meant that no accountability, reporting system, or job descriptions were developed. We were now financially a part of the hospital but we still had no formal structural connection with the other professional staff.

2. Changes

While the Case Aide program was becoming part of the state hospital system, other changes were occurring that had a substantial impact on the program. The first such change, in June of 1970, was the unitization of the hospital. "Unitization" was the term used to describe the division of the hospital into three smaller hospitals, or units, as they were called. This reorganization of the hospital meant a re-assignment of staff, as well as patients, to different wards. A new structure was evolving within the hospital, existing in some cases side by side with the old departments or in other cases, superseding them. The "unit" actually encompassed all the services of the hospital organized to serve the needs of a particular geographic area. Patients were now assigned to wards based on their place of residence prior to admission. These hospital units were ideally designed to be supplemental to corresponding area comprehensive community mental health centers. It should be noted, however, that, of the three hospital units, only one had an existing mental health facility in the community; a second was in the slow process of development; and the third had nothing. The areas were economically and ethnically quite diverse, ranging from high income suburbs to urban, ghetto-styled flop houses.

Unitization, as stated above, impacted strongly on the Case

Aide program as it was then organized. It still had the responsibility to serve all the patients wherever they might have lived, and so had to work together with all three of the geographic units, plus diverse other special services. Since each of these units now serviced differing populations, the Case Aide program had to begin negotiations with each of the units separately and to respond to the particular patients, needs, and philosophies of each. At the same time, we tried to continue in our ambiguous relationship to the social service department in the old departmental structure, so as not to antagonize this director.

Each of these units was headed by a psychiatrist. Our program was staffed totally by social workers, who were considered less important in the hospital hierarchy. Thus, in these necessary negotiations, the Case Aide program was always operating from a different, and inferior, power base. The role of the social service director, to whom the staff of the Case Aide program ostensibly reported, became more and more nebulous as the three unit directors (i.e. psychiatrists) emerged as the "powers" within the new organization.

As noted above, the original director of the Case Aide program had resigned prior to the change-over to state control and unitization. The two social workers who remained each had her own program and conducted her own negotiations with unit staff. Eventually, one of these two social workers also left the program. This move left Barbara, who had been with the program consistently since a few months after its inception in 1965.

The hiring of a replacement—another Case Aide supervisor—was an interesting phenomenon. Who was responsible for hiring now? The remaining social worker (Barbara)?—the Case Aide Board?—the director of social service?—the hospital personnel department? Since no one seemed ready to do anything, Barbara began to create the pattern that would characterize the program for the remainder of its life span. She stepped into the power vacuum; Barbara, in conjunction with the social service director who acted as liaison with the hospital personnel department, hired Cathy in record time for a state organization. Four days transpired between interview and starting date. The Case Aide Board was not involved in this process. Since Cathy did not meet the board until several months after being hired, and did not fully understand its historical significance to the program, seeds were sown for an authority conflict later.

The working relationship that began to develop, almost from our first meeting, was a joy for both of us. In addition to this good working relationship, we found that we genuinely liked and respected each other. Our talents and skills were unusually complementary; Barbara's ability to relate and involve immediately, plus Cathy's head for long range planning and evaluation, enabled us both to build on one another's skills. Co-leadership became the modality of choice and we conceived of the Case Aide program for the first time as an administrative whole. We implemented this conception by co-leadership of groups, administrative planning meetings, and the collection of statistical data.

During the latter part of 1970 and the early months of 1971, conflict developed between the staff and the board. We disagreed over these key issues.

1. The ratio of patients to volunteers: to this point in the history of the program, the one-to-one relationship had been used exclusively. For each patient referred to the program, there had to be one volunteer. As long as the program remained small, the supervision of these several individual Case Aide/patient relationships remained manageable. However, after unitization of the hospital with its subsequent upheaval, more and more patients were being referred for Case Aide services. If we continued to add volunteers to meet the increased demand, the amount of supervisory time needed could not be provided by the present staff. Since there was no possibility of increasing the paid supervisory staff, we wanted to experiment with both Case Aide-led patient groups, as well as having the more experienced Case Aides function in a supervisory capacity with the newer, incoming volunteers.

2. Administrative whole vs. separation of supervisors: as noted above, we had already begun to pull the various pieces of the program together—evaluating where it had been and where we felt it should be going. We found that much of our time had to be devoted to the administration of the operation—a program piece that had been neglected since the program's inception. The Case Aide board had difficulty recognizing the validity of time spent in this manner and wanted to continue the previous practice of each supervisor having her own separate program. We, on the other hand, needed the unity of purpose and procedure in order to function most efficiently; and, quite frankly, we did not want to turn administrative planning over to the board again. They had given up some of the power reins through attrition once the program came under state fiscal control.

3. The type of volunteer to be recruited: was the third issue that caused a divergence of opinion. Not only were an increased number of patients being referred to us, but also different kinds of patients. After unitization, more staff began to recognize the helpfulness of the Case Aide in a patient's readiness for discharge. They asked us to accept younger patients, those with more acute problems, those who were judged hopelessly institutionalized, and to bring the Case Aide relationship both further into the back wards and also out into the community to prevent hospitalizations. We found that we needed a variety of Case Aides in order to respond to these new patients as, for example, college students who could provide adolescents with the all-important healthy peer identification so lacking in hospital life. In addition, the program had to be extended into the evening hours to be responsive to the working patient who desperately needed support at this crucial time, and, consequently, we needed career men and women who were familiar with the working world. As helpful as the housewife was—she was the initial Case Aide—we decided that the program should also offer newer and additional services via a variety of volunteers.

The above issues were the battleground; however, we feel that the real war was fought over the role of the board in the future of the program. We felt—and still feel—that tremendous respect and credit are due to these board members for creating, initiating, funding, and advertising the Case Aide program in the first place. Yet, their role needed to become different and more reflective of the changes that were occuring both inside and outside the program-state funding, organizational changes in the hospital, and the hiring by the hospital of a new staff member—Cathy. However, the staff and the board had reached an impasse. Unable to resolve these differences, the board chose to resign in April 1973, thus withdrawing their support.

3. *Decisions*

The resignation of the Case Aide Board forced us to make several important decisions. The Case Aide program was now without community sanction; we were also without any real hospital sanction as evinced by the board's initial negotiations with the hospital and the system's subsequent lack of response to the program. Therefore, we were alone. We had several alternatives:

1. turn ourselves over to one of the hospital's geographical units to gain a hospital identity. The major drawbacks in this plan were the limitations imposed on the population that we would be able to serve and the loss of our newly found autonomy.
2. attempt to find another community "mother". Again, we found that we did not want to sacrifice our autonomy nor undertake the enormous task of soliciting such support. We did organize a broad, loosely structured "auxiliary" of present and former Case Aides and other interested people who helped to raise money and to recruit new volunteers.

We found that we were in a unique position. We owed allegiance to no one. Nothing interfered with our two priorities which were providing patients with effective service and to enable Case Aides to make a significant contribution. So, we decided to go it alone. We wanted to use this opportunity to test out theories of treatment, supervision, and administration. We had no idea how long we could survive in the hospital system. We realized that we had to create a structure to meet the needs of an independent operation. We had to conceive of ourselves as administrators, as well as social workers. One of our first administrative decisions was that we needed consultation services from a business/management expert. We obtained such help from the Harvard Business School in return for allowing our unit to be a case study in the management of non-profit operations. This consultation helped us to separate out the emotional issues and to put our history into perspective. As a Program, we were able to clarify what our problems were, what our strengths were, and what our weaknesses were so that we could design an administrative system to more effectively meet our objectives.

Because in the past the Program had had diverse part-time social workers operating separately without a unity of philosophy or practice, the image of the program throughout the hospital reflected these different personalities. There also was a great deal of fragmentation within the program which had resulted from trying to be all things to all people. We felt that the resolution of the problem had to begin with the Case Aide program identity. We arrived at this construct by a complete re-evaluation of the total operation . . . piece by piece.

The Case Aide: Who was the Case Aide? Who volunteered and why? Where from and for how long? Did they meet the needs of the program? What were the tasks that they performed? What was the time involved? What was the time that we had to invest in them? Was it justified? Why did they leave after a year's commitment? Why did they stay?

The Patient: How did he come to our attention? For what purpose? What happened to him? Was there a particular person who best utilized our service? What was the service that we offered? How many could we service? For how long? What was our responsibility after discharge?

The Hospital: How was our program viewed? Who used it? And why? Which disciplines? What was the staff investment after the referral? How was the role of the Case Aide perceived? What was the relationship between the Case Aide and the staff? What was the role of the Case Aide supervisors vis à vis the staff?

The Case Aide Supervisor: What was our relationship to the patient? To the Case Aide? To the staff? To the community? What was the investment of our time in the above areas? Could we determine priorities among these various components?

The initial phase of the development of our plan was a re-evaluation of the Case Aides themselves. They were the basic resource of the Program and we felt that we had to begin there. We talked to each Case Aide who had been in the program for longer than one year, involving them in the planning process. One issue that became immediately apparent was that the previous organizational structure had not allowed for enough continuing growth and development. Since the modality had been the one-to-one relationship exclusively, a significant number of Case Aides who had been in the program for approximately three years had only repeated their initial experience over and over. Though they had demonstrated an effectiveness in the individual treatment relationship, their wealth of skills was not being extended both qualitatively and quantitatively. We felt that they could be enabled to learn more diverse treatment skills in addition to extending our reach to many more patients.

We wanted to expand the service that we offered without increasing appreciably the personnel. We felt that we could accomplish this goal, as well as the stimulation and re-vitalization of these senior Case Aides, by the development of a "new dimensions" program. These new dimensions included training in group leadership, co-therapy, peer supervision, network intervention, community consultation, and program development. Not only did we want to train these Case Aides for specific tasks helpful to us here and now, but also we wanted to see such skills carried back into their own communities and put to work in a variety of creative ways.

This new dimensions program led to a development of various performance levels among the Case Aide population;

1. we had new Case Aides who were doing individual and traditional work;
2. we had Case Aides who were involved in individual short-term situations, small informal group activities, such as breakfast parties, movie dates, shopping trips, etc., and other special projects;
3. we had senior Case Aides carrying multiple individual situations;
4. we had senior Case Aides leading therapy groups;
5. we had senior Case Aides involved in a series of community and/or hospital consultations.

Concomitantly, we had to develop new teaching materials, as well as different supervisory schedules.

Another variable of the game plan was recruiting and scheduling. We found that the majority of our Case Aides came from only one of the three geographic areas that the hospital serviced. In order to keep the program relevant, we aimed our recruitment at selective towns. As a result, we were able to attract enough Case Aides to fill three seminar groups that corresponded to the three hospital units. We were able to assign Case Aides from particular towns to patients who were former residents of those same towns and who would be returning to them after discharge.

We made several other decisions about Case Aides that were important to the quality of the program. We recruited graduate and undergraduate students in addition to the more traditional "mature" volunteers. There were certain accommodations that we had to make, such as our availability in the evenings and the acceptance of the academic, rather than calendar, year to fulfill the commitment. Thus, we were able to reach out to a more diverse patient population, including more male patients, younger patients needing a peer relationship, and working patients who were on the road to recovery, who needed additional support, and for whom no one had been available before.

We also developed a measuring system for the input of Case Aide time on particular tasks vis à vis our input time. In addition, we found that within one year we doubled the number of patients in the program without significantly changing the number of Case Aides; we halved the amount of time that we spent in supervision, without sacrificing the quality of that supervision. We were able to expand our own services in other directions—research, community education, and program planning and evaluation.

Our first decision—to remain autonomous—implied that we would also remain separate from the rest of the hospital. Being "separate" meant that we were on our own, for better or for worse. We were physically isolated, philosophically alien, and utterly outside the system. We decided to turn this isolation and lack of sanction into an advantage vis à vis the hospital; separate, we could maintain our professional integrity and fight for good patient care. We felt that we had a better perspective on the reality of patient living than those who were more incorporated into the system. We tried to tell the truth to both the volunteers and to the patients. To say the least, we found upsetting the placid acceptance of hospital conditions by most of the staff: "It's better than it was", or "You'll get used to it"!

Although we were separate, we did want to develop positive relationships and some modes of communication with the rest of the staff—both professional and non-professional. Our communication network revolved around two needs:

1. to sell our "product" and

2. to obtain the material that we needed in order to operate.

Since we were not permanently appointed to our positions under civil service, we were outside any administrative reporting system. Therefore, we developed our own job descriptions, program evaluations, and administrative accounting systems in order to keep our heads above water and to justify our existence in hospital terms (as we understood them).

In order to operate at all, we had to get on the supply train. When we took up residence at the hospital, we were assigned an unused ward—no desks, no chairs, no typewriter, no nothing. Being "passive" got us absolutely nowhere; but by being aggressive, visible, and persistent, documenting any and all requests, we got nearly everything. Using the mechanics of the system against the administrative morass, we managed to get supplies and earned the grudging respect of the steward who was forced by our persistence and ingenuity to deal with us.

If we got on the supply train by nastiness, we stayed on through courtesy. Thank you letters, public recognition of help, and involvement of maintenance staff in the helping process interested them in our program and maintained their assistance. For example, the telephone operators knew that we would help with calls that they did not know what to do with; the janitorial staff became interested in teaching some of our patients cleaning and maintenance skills that could prepare them for outside employment; the kitchen staff became involved in preparing picnic lunches for patient outings; and, even the steward, tight-fisted as he was, gave us enough coffee to continuously satisfy all our Case Aides and patients.

In addition, since we were responsible for patients from all the hospital service areas, we had to negotiate with each of the geographical units separately—each with their separate problems and philosophies—tailoring our dealings with each in order to have our service accepted by all. But, most especially, so that the service was accepted by the nurses who were our major source of access to patients.

4. Demise:

So far, we have discussed these changes in the Case Aide program from 1965-1973:

1. began as a small, community based, "female" volunteer program, privately funded, with a strong community board

and a tenuous relationship to the state hospital system;
2. the program doubled in numbers maintaining its original structure, but with changes in the Case Aide staff;
3. external forces, such as unitization and the loss of its private funding source, force the program to become hospitally sponsored;
4. new staff (Cathy) and an internal re-evaluation tried to make the program more responsive to the changing needs of the hospital population;
5. the board resigned, leaving the program without community sanction and with only a financial relationship to the large hospital structure;
6. the program was re-organized; it now included two full time co-directors (who were social workers) and a variety of relevant Case Aide seminar groups.

Fifteen months later, the Case Aide program was closed down —both of the authors had resigned—and less than 10% of the Case Aides remained. What happened and why?

It is extremely hard for us to be objective about the demise of the program. We have swung from hysteria, to anger, to guilt, to "we told us so", back to hysteria, anger and guilt. With time, we can separate out various factors that contributed:

1. hospital climate at the time;
2. our own contributions;
3. specific triggering events.

During the fifteen months of independent operation, we were in high gear. Our negotiations with hospital units were quite effective since we shared, for perhaps the first time, a common mandate. Unitization's purpose was the de-institutionalization of the hospital's population. We had been highly successful in this area; therefore, Case Aide services were in demand since we had demonstrated an expertise in this area over the past seven years of the program's life.

It is important to review the demise of the program in terms of our own contributions to it. To begin with, we had decided to try it alone, without the sanction of any one community or hospital group. Our own autonomy had provided us with the freedom to develop, experiment, and to invest all of our energies in this program. We had, in the process, alienated some community members and hospital staff. Another factor that must be considered is that the very qualities that enabled us to be so effective with patients and Case Aides—visible, brash, honest, persistent, confronting—were the very same qualities that seemed to create a high discomfort level in some other hospital personnel. Although we had seemingly been pursuing the same goals as the administration, we had lost sight of an important and subterranean issue: if the goal of de-hospitalization were achieved in the near future, the hospital would be closed and many of the staff would be jobless. Thus, there was a tremendous ambivalence that we personally did not feel, but that was strongly felt by older employees who were so close to "safe" retirement. We had been lulled into a false security based on positive results.

The actual triggering event of the confrontation between the program and the hospital occurred when a new director of the social service department was hired. He came into a job position that still contained some latent power which he chose to use to strengthen the social work input in the hospital. One of his administrative decisions was to diffuse the viability of the Case Aide program throughout the department. We agreed with his basic premise; however, he chose to accomplish this task by the incorporation of the program. We felt that its "separateness" and "specialness" were its greatest strengths. We had begun moving toward closer unit liaisons, but we had insisted on the autonomous operation of the program. He felt that the program's autonomy interfered with staff interrelations.

We, on the other hand, felt that we did not need, nor did we want, to be a "part" of the hospital system; we had demonstrated the ability to deliver an effective service *because* we were separate. The new director felt that we were effective *in spite of* our separateness.

Therefore, control of the program—by us, or by the hospital—became an issue, non-negotiable by both parties. There was no question that he had the power and the approval of the hospital. After all, we were saying that we did not want to be part of "it"; "it" would not stand for that. We had gotten away with such an attitude as long as it was not overt. Once the conflict was stated, we may have been right, but we were "out".

Since there was no way that we, as program directors, could survive this control issue, we spent our last three months at the hospital negotiating on behalf of patients and Case Aides in an attempt to make the incorporation of the Case Aide program as constructive as possible:

1. We offered consulting services to social service staff members on the units who had been designated as the new Case Aide supervisors, sharing with them the guidelines that we had developed for recruiting, screening, matching, and supervising the volunteers; unfortunately, those designated to take over these responsibilities were angry but only passively resistant, not towards us, but towards the director, who was burdening them with extra work, and thus they were unwilling and sometimes unable to handle this new role.
2. Concomitantly, we tried to define and delineate the basic issues and implications of the structural changes to the Case Aides and their patients. We had an ethical responsibility to bring out all sides of the conflict so that Case Aides, patients, community and hospital could all have an opportunity to re-structure the program. While our own positions were intractable, we hoped that much of the program's essence could be salvaged. Apathy, however, overpowered the situation once we were gone, and there was no support from any community group to "watchdog" the future administration of such a program. We are no longer at the hospital; "grapevine" has it that the program has become institutionalized, sinking back into the sea of hospital bureaucracy, and there are no more waves to cause discomfort and change. One patient, hospitalized for many years, but now out and enjoying life thanks to the Case Aide program, summarized many of our feelings when she remarked wistfully, "I should have known that anything as good as this program couldn't survive."

CHAPTER VII
BRING ON THE DANCERS: THE FALLOUT

As the drowning person sees with clarity a myriad of marvellous memories and moments, so do we see this last year flash before our eyes. 1972-1973 was truly the apex of the Case Aide Program—a wealth of quality Case Aides doing quality work which resulted in 50% of 120 patients leaving the hospital in less than a year. Here is an example of our weekly calendar:

1. Sixty patients being seen individually by Case Aides;
2. Five groups of Case Aides meeting with the Supervisors on four different mornings and one evening.
3. Individual supervision—approximately 22 Case Aides for each supervisor.
4. Sixty patients being seen in eight different groups at regular weekly times on the Case Aide floor—all eight groups led by two or more Case Aides.
5. The eight teams of group leaders of patient groups receiving intensive supervision of their work, both in individual weekly conferences and in bi-monthly seminar meetings.
6. Supervisors attending at least one staff meeting of hospital unit personnel per week.
7. Supervisors also involved in writing, community meetings, publicity, consultations, telephone calls, planning

of seminars, recruiting, screening, etc.

8. Community groups, dance and music groups, and others.

The Case Aide Unit was rarely quiet: there was always a buzz of voices, laughter, people coming and going; food being prepared or eaten in the kitchen; the smell of coffee, a dog barking happily when a familiar form came into view . . . a true sense of vitality and purpose.

The positive feelings being generated by Case Aides, patients, and ourselves resulted in a spiraling of new activities and new dimensions for the program. It might be simpler to use an historical order to describe the diverse new programs and projects that evolved over the eight years of the program's life. Each of these satellites developed a personality and often a life of its own, but all were in response to the needs of the hospital population.

I FAMILY CARE:

The first of these programs was Family Care, mentioned briefly in Chapter 2, which was as an alternative to hospitalization. When we first began working at the hospital, we really did not anticipate the possibility of long-hospitalized people leaving the hospital. Our initial goal was to help improve the life quality of these people, to bring them some friendliness, to re-introduce them to a more "normal life". Even after a few months of Case Aide visits, we noticed remarkable changes in people's appearances and attitudes; and, we soon realized that we had a responsibility to take the next step with those who were ready . . . a move out of the hospital and into the community. In some instances, a nursing home was a satisfactory placement if the individual were quite elderly and possibly had some physical infirmity. In other situations, the person was too young and too active to fit into such an environment. What then? We learned from discussions with other state facilities, as well as from the administrator of this hospital, that there was already a foster home department in the Department of Mental Health that provided money and guidelines for the establishment of state foster homes for adults, as well as children. In this particular hospital, this funding had not been used nor had any administrative structure been established to find the homes and supervise them. For almost two years a volunteer filled this position under the supervision of the Case Aide Program's two social workers. This particular lady was uniquely qualified; she was a retired psychiatric nurse who was also very active in church and community work. Together, we did the publicity to attract people to this kind of job, that of welcoming former mental patients into their homes. Via newspaper articles, speaking engagements, radio and T-V spots, and informal contacts, we managed to find the initial eight homes that received more than a dozen men and women during the first year of the Family Care Program. The volunteer nurse visited each home several times with the prospective resident so that the families and new resident could get acquainted. We had a formal screening process for these foster families to determine their sincerity and ability to deal with former mental patients; we also provided on-going support both from the nurse and from the Case Aide staff. We made every effort to make a good "match" between the home and the special resident. Over the years, we learned a great deal about the qualities that proved to be most important for good family care homes, and we also learned that whenever possible, it was best to place more than one patient in each new home. Good family care homes often involved people who were accustomed to a large family, people who had a need to be helpful to others, or who were lonely, or who had experienced illness themselves, either directly or via another family member. There was a financial need met and formal guidelines established which helped to protect both parties in this arrangement. We provided social services and medical services to the ex-patient as well as a modest financial stipend every month. In return, we expected that the foster parents would provide a decent room, with no more than two persons to a room, adequate meals, and laundry facilities. We generally tried to find homes that were neither isolated from community facilities nor far from good transportation so that it would be possible for these residents to get out by themselves and with friends. We found that when two or three people moved out together or within months of one another, the adjustment was much easier. There was a real rapport among people who had shared the hospital experience.

Naturally, there were good homes, adequate ones, and bad homes. We had, on some occasions, to move patients into other homes. Of course, there were similar contrasts in the individual's ability to deal with his new home and new "family". Some could adapt amazingly fast to a whole different set of values, customs and expectations. Others had more difficulty and needed more support and more time to make the leap. John B., who had been hospitalized for 45 years had some problems adapting to his first "home". He was accustomed to getting up at 6 a.m. and now was living with a retired couple who slept 'til 9 a.m. They were annoyed to hear him whistling in the shower at such an early hour. When we got together to talk about the conflicts on both sides, these little problems were ironed out as each became more understanding and considerate of the other. They needed to learn more about John's former life to appreciate what it meant to him to sleep in a room with only one other man, to be able to use the toilet alone and shave and shower when he felt like it or needed it, to eat at flexible times, and to be able to go into a kitchen and have a cup of coffee—not only at meal times. John also had to learn to use the most common of household tools, such as an electric can opener, blender, modern stove and oven, and the washing machine and dryer. Fortunately, Mr. and Mrs. Smith were understanding and had a good sense of humor, as did John: so, they learned to live together. Like several other foster parents, they soon invited two other men to join them. John became their assistant in helping these newcomers to "learn the ropes" as he had. And, after two years, John moved out into his own apartment, supporting himself with a part-time job and his social security benefits.

John was more fortunate than many other people who had been hospitalized for so much of their adult life; he had marketable skills and had been working for a number of years before he moved out of the hospital. Most of the people that we dealt with had no financial resources at all—they were penniless. The Family Care Program did not provide any money for the ex-patient, only a monthly payment ($7.50 per patient per day) to the foster parents. Thus, most of our clients were totally without resources, unless they were lucky enough to find some limited employment in the community that they lived in. For most of them, though, finding and keeping a job was extremely difficult since they had not had any job training or experience in a number of years. Also, there was frequently a lot of discrimination within these small towns against the stranger from the state hospital. It was frustrating for many of our ex-patients to have no money and to be exposed, for the first time in years, to all the consumer merchandise and services that are now available, such as beauty parlors, stores, restaurants. Again, the Case Aide Program took on another responsibility—that of providing money, or helping to find jobs, or pleading clients' cases to community resources.

One important development that we have not touched upon was the administrative changes that occurred in Family Care over the years. After the Case Aide program had demonstrated the effectiveness of this type of housing, as well as having provided the homes, the Family Care Program was integrated into the nursing department of the hospital. We worked with the nursing supervisor who was assigned to this position during the next two years. Although our relationship was informal, it was pleasant and efficient. We continued to help find homes via our publicity and community contacts as well as to screen the homes and match the patients to the appropriate families. The nurse was responsible for the medical follow-up, the contacts with the family care "parents", and was the liaison between the patient and the hospital. In cooperation with the Case Aide, who usually remained involved for at least several months, the nurse also made the necessary community contacts for the patients—job referrals, etc.

Unfortunately, in the next four years of this program, there were four different nurses and each one interpreted her role quite differently. Because there was no strong leadership from the Director of Nursing, whose own role had changed considerably, the family care nurses were without support or supervision. They also became involved with other tasks in the hospital itself and devoted less and less of their time to the family care homes and the patients living in them. So, the number of homes remained small and the lives of the patients remained static. It was extremely frustrating for us to see a potentially viable alternative to hospitalization just stagnate.

Yet, we had no administrative responsibility, so there was little that we could do to remedy the situation.

II. ALLOWANCES

The allowance program grew out of the need for patients in family care to have some money of their own. It soon became an independent structure, with its own volunteer staff, bank account, and some administrative ties to the Case Aide Program. Each year, money was raised by church groups, student organizations, and patients, which was used for monthly allowances for those people both in the hospital and in foster homes who had no other resources. Although the amount was small—generally $5-$10 per month—it was the difference between penury and pride. For some people, it meant paying for a movie or pack of cigarettes themselves or treating a friend to a cup of coffee, instead of constantly having to accept the charity of others. Most of the recipients of these monies were eager to repay it or to contribute to the fund when they eventually got a job. Each year, a sufficient sum of money was also raised to provide holiday gifts for every client of the Case Aide program, as well as a large, festive party that was usually hosted by some community group.

III. SOCIALIZATION PROGRAM

Almost spontaneously, another satellite program developed that was the social group which we will call the "Jollies". As people began to move into the community from the state hospital, whether they moved into nursing homes, family care homes, individual rooms or apartments, or their own family home, there was still a social gap. Their relationship to their Case Aide and, to a lesser degree, to diverse community groups, was only the first step in the re-integration to a "normal" social life. Many of these people did not know how, or were afraid to try, to make social contacts on their own and sat waiting in their rooms and homes for a Case Aide visit. Some were fortunate enough to have some friends or relatives who had remained interested in them during their hospitalization or who had renewed their relationships when they left the hospital. Others too were fortunate in that their foster parents included them in their own social life. But for the majority, there was the emptiness of the new place and many adjustments, but no one to share these experiences with or to learn from.

A few Case Aides became conscious of this need and started getting together on a weekly basis with their particular patient friends and a few other patients and Case Aides who were also interested. Soon, the program grew into a well-organized club with a volunteer director and assistants; these marvellous volunteers have met weekly with 10-20 patients for seven years. Some of the original volunteers and ex-patients are still in this club adding new members yearly and even raising small funds to help support themselves. The membership includes both people in and out of the hospital and has been extremely helpful in bridging the gap between hospitalization and communitization. Over the years, they have done a variety of things together. They have taken courses in sewing and ceramics, gone to baseball games and the theater, and given luncheons for one another on special occasions. And each year, they hold a reunion at the beach home of the original volunteer director. The relationship of this club to the Case Aide program has been close but informal. Although initially we helped to "staff" it, support it and fund it, it soon became independent and developed its own organizational structure and relied only on the Case Aide program to make patient referrals and to provide some help in dealing with hospital staff. Another important dimension of this social group was the consultation service it had provided to other agencies who became interested in offering similar services in their own communites. It has been a very gratifying experience to see other social clubs for ex-patients cropping up in three other areas of the state, after our staff and that of the "Jollies" met with personnel in these places.

The value of each of these projects went beyond the direct services they offered. The more subtle effect of all of them was the educational process that occurred. Many more citizens became involved with mental illness via our efforts to obtain foster homes, allowances, and social experience for the mentally ill. Even people who could not or would not become directly involved could feel the satisfaction of helping by buying a raffle ticket or attending a church sponsored social for patients. This kind of community involvement had far-reaching consequences in terms of positive and non-threatening contacts with mental hospitals and mental illness. People who could not give of themselves, or their time, gave money, ideas, and often job and educational resources that we might not have had access to without these broader contacts in the community, via fund-raising and social clubs.

The following sections are descriptions of projects, listed here in the order they evolved within the larger program.

IV. MUSIC THERAPY

Music classes, conducted by a Case Aide who was also a talented pianist and music teacher, started when she played the piano for patients on the wards. Later, she was invited to work with children in who had not responded to more traditional modes of therapy. After a number of years as a volunteer working with dozens of withdrawn and disturbed boys and girls, she recently became a paid staff therapist working with other personnel on a full-time basis. Her work is considered to be important and effective, and she has provided consulting services throughout the state.

V. CLOTHING BOUTIQUE

A clothing boutique was the result of a local high school's concern for the mentally ill in this near-by state hospital. These young people, under our supervision, worked one day a week on the Case Aide Unit. They built clothing racks, solicited attractive, clean clothing, and staffed the "Boutique" so that patients could look at clothing in a private and attractive setting. They hung up mirrors and made cute dressing rooms and even provided simple alterations. In addition to the real service they provided, there was also the vitality, friendliness, and joy that they brought to all the people they met on their weekly visits. As one patient said, "I don't really need any more clothes, I just enjoy coming up and having a cup of coffee with those cheerful kids".

VI. THE DANCERS

A unique group that deserves special mention is the Dance Group that was conducted by some college students. Based on their dance training and a summer dance therapy experience at a state mental hospital in another state, they offered to develop a similar dance program for a limited number of chronic patients. It was their feeling, and ours too, that one of the gravest problems of the long term hospitalized person is too little exercise—compounded with a starchy diet, over-heated wards and enervating boredom.

Therefore, we carefully negotiated with one of the Unit directors and the Director of Nursing to gain access to one of the neglected back wards for the dancers. The ward offered to us was all men, mostly middle-aged or elderly. We suspected that the staff was saying, "Take these rejects; you can't do any real harm and probably no visible good."

Two nights a week of 45-minute dance sessions for 40 weeks did 12 men a lot of good and did the same for the two therapists and a score of friends who often came along to join in and enjoy! Admittedly, the fact that all the dancers were extremely attractive and lively young people could have been effective in itself, but, very obviously, moving, touching, and expressing with their rusty, stolid bodies was a new and exhilarating feeling for these men. To see men who had formerly shuffled with their eyes down now look at one another, and jump, touch their toes, and take responsibility for new steps and motions, was an exciting and rewarding experience for all of us.

As a result of careful planning and lengthy meetings with the hospital administrators, we were able to gain permission to videotape some of the dance sessions. Our purpose was not only to provide the patients with a concrete validation of their identity and their activity, but also to provide the hospital with a vivid record (and teaching tool) of an innovative example of non-verbal communication.

VII. A LEGAL ASSISTANCE PROGRAM

A nearby university organized this program, in which law students volunteered to give free legal advice to hospitalized patients. Our initial contacts with these students involved collaboration on particular cases with which we were involved as well.

As we discussed several patients, it became apparent to all of us that there was a gap in the knowledge of both groups. While the lawyers were unfamiliar with both the hospital system and what mental illness meant to the patients, we, on the other hand, as social workers, had only superficial understanding of the patients' civil rights. In order to provide a better service to our clients, we developed a formal consultation/collaboration between the two disciplines.

During the previous year, the laws governing the incarceration of the mentally ill had changed drastically, and there was a communication gap. You see, few staff people took the initiative to inform patients, for example, that they had a *right* to make phone calls to certain people, such as their attorney, physician, or clergyman. Of course, there were no free phones for this purpose, but, at least, the statute was on the books. Patients had some negotiating power.

Again, civil rights were not exactly our bailiwick, but not only do patients have rights, but they also have a right to *know* that they have rights. We tried to provide a climate, in our program, where issues such as mistreatment by staff, lack of medical or psychiatric attention, and family and financial difficulties could be discussed without fear of reprisal and with some hope of redress.

VIII. THE TEMPLE GROUP

Concurrent with some of the projects that we have already described were our consultations with several church and temple groups. They were interested in learning how to develop meaningful volunteer projects in the hospital because they had tried working with the volunteer department but had found the director vague, unavailable, and generally unresponsive.

Along with certain members of the nursing staff, we helped to organize holiday visits to churches and temples, as well as special interest programs, such as excursions by patient groups to attend local concerts, art exhibits, theatre productions and other activities.

A specific example of satellite community programs was the Temple Group, which developed from the interest of a Case Aide who was very involved in her local temple. This Case Aide was in the unique position of being able to evaluate certain of the needs of two "populations"—her colleagues in the temple and the patients in the hospital. She approached us to arrange a series of organizational meetings in our Unit. At the first meeting of this potential group, approximately ten residents of the Jewish community participated. It soon became apparent that their goals were quite disparate, ranging from the purely religious purpose of worship shared by the Jewish patient population and Jewish community residents, to the goals of a more social and therapeutic project.

We arranged a contract with them to help clarify their goals, to structure their organization, and to utilize hospital resources. These tasks were accomplished in eight subsequent meetings. They had, by then, identified the Jewish population of the hospital, developed and arranged a consistent Sabbath program consisting of both religious and social aspects, and had become a positive and recognizable resource to the hospital staff. Thus, they became an established volunteer program independent from us. The second stage of the consultation that we provided was twofold:

1. ongoing case consultations, concerning specific patients with whom they were involved, within the framework of generalized mental health practice and techniques;

2. liaison work between the group and the hospital system. In all actuality, our role was that of intervener or facilitator. Because of our established identity as social workers for "volunteers" within the hospital and within the communities, we were visible and accessible for them. We confirmed such a role by reinforcing and supporting their project and also sharing our extensive knowledge of resources throughout the state. This positive experience encouraged similar groups, such as church groups, high school programs, etc., to reach out to us

for guidance in organizing a variety of other social and recreational projects.

IX. SAM

We have not yet really discussed "Sam, the Dachshund's" role in the Case Aide Unit. Aside from being a constant and loving companion for her owner Barbara and a loyal friend to Cathy, Sam became a symbol of humor, "homey"-ness, as well as the general all-round Case Aide pet. One psychotic young girl could only talk to her Case Aide through Sam initially. One mute man said his first "hello" to this dog, and many others enjoyed touching her, feeding her, and being greeted by her. She was little, she was soft, and she was ever-loving and undemanding. She seemed to meet many needs and elicited incredibly important material about people's identity, memories, and feelings. One patient group, as we have already discussed in Chapter 5, adopted her for Thursday mornings and even named their group "Sam's Early Birds".

Since noticing Sam's exceptional ability to be an "amateur psychiatrist", we have learned that some mental hospitals in the West are using dogs, especially with children, as part of the treatment team. Animals can teach all of us the basic elements of love; they don't want to love you "because of . . . ", or "if you do . . . ", which has been the experience of most frightened and mentally ill people. They just want to love you because "you're you". Animals can also allow very regressed patients to cuddle, to stroke another living thing, to return to their most intimate relationships, while still behaving in an "appropriate" manner, whatever that might be!

X. THE CASE AIDE CHRONICLE

Sam also graced the front page of our *Case Aide Chronicle,* a quarterly newsletter. Our purpose was to provide a "voice" for the people involved in the Unit; we printed poems and articles by patients and Case Aides, and a review of our current events such as who left the hospital, who got a job, who was accepted into graduate school, etc. Just newsy mimeographed sheets of paper to communicate within the hospital and in the community that there were some real live people here in the hospital doing some normal, fun things—not weird, frightening people to match the strange sounding diagnostic words, like "schizoid, paranoid, etc." The patients, Case Aides, and community residents were pleased and proud of the paper. Yet, typical of the hospital staff, they called up to ask why we had not mentioned them in some way, although we were mentioning people or events as they became relevant to our particular unit. One nurse was actually furious with us because, since we had described our holiday festivities, she felt that we were implying that the Case Aide unit was the only unit that ever "did" anything for patients. We carefully explained that ours was not a general hospital newspaper and that we could only comment on what our unit did. We suggested that she develop a newspaper for her unit of the hospital . . . to no avail . . .

Eventually, we concluded that the hard work on the newsletter was resulting in worse communications, rather than better, and that we were becoming too painfully visible. The more the hospital staff "saw" us and "heard" us, the more separate and vulnerable we became—developing into objects of jealousy, fear, misunderstanding, and distrust.

XI. APARTMENT GROUP

Next in our historic perspective is the Apartment Group that began soon after our development of other Case Aide-led patient groups. This project was a response to a specific need that we had become aware of—the lack of alternatives available to people leaving the hospital. We had already initiated an evening group of Case Aides who, for the most part, were matched up with patients who were employed or in work training programs or educational programs. Realizing that these clients would eventually need a place to live convenient to their place of employment, we invited an interested staff social worker and an experienced "senior" Case Aide, to start an evening group with seven women who were without individual Case Aides and who were employed or who had good potential for both a job and discharge from the hospital in the near future. Our hope was to help these people who had spent from 1-20 years in the hospital to form a supportive relationship which would then be transferrable to a living situation outside the hospital.

This group met weekly, and very quickly a warm and constructive relationship developed among the members and leaders; they talked about job concerns, social problems, preferred places to live, and also learned together how to plan budgets, how to shop and plan menus, and then, how to cook. They went bowling together and apartment-hunting too. Within four months of their first meeting, they had found a 3-bedroom place, and four of the women were ready to move in and able to pay their own way. Their happiness and excitement was contagious; it was also an inspiration for other patients and Case Aides, as well as a real "first" for the hospital. Up until this time, the hospitalized could only turn to family care, isolated boarding house rooms, nursing homes, and a few family situations.

As with so many of these Case Aide "spin-off" projects, the apartment group provided another opportunity for community involvement. To help the ladies in their new venture, we held a raffle to raise extra money. This money helped to pay the first month's rent, purchased some needed furniture, and was a little financial "cushion" for this courageous group. The Case Aides and other community friends got together and had an "apartment shower"; hospital staff was invited too, and it was a festive occasion. Everyone brought some little household item—potholders, dishes, towels and sheets, etc. . . . some new, some used, some hand-made. Patients, volunteers, families, and staff mingled on this occasion. Although several professional staff members were openly dubious, the ladies have been in their same cozy apartment for more than a year, surviving illnesses, job losses, and other normal ups and downs.

Almost as important as the success of these four ladies is the courage it gave other patients and staff members to develop other apartment projects. There are now two of these homes, with others planned.

XII. WORKSHOPS

In conjunction with our consulting and publicity projects, we planned the first of two Case Aide conferences in the state. The effectiveness of this particular volunteer program, especially in relation to the institutionalized person, had attracted the attention of the state volunteer community mental health association. For two years, we planned and hosted a state-wide meeting of volunteer groups who were also involved with services to the mentally ill.

BEFORE THE FALL:

The chapter began at the ending, in a sense. We have described in these pages the activities of the Case Aide Program in the last year of its "life". We also worked backward in subsequent pages to discuss the numerous satellite programs that evolved over the years in response to the needs of the Case Aides' clients. Many of these projects became independent and have expanded and reached into other areas and have taken on new forms. Some are still providing services to their original clients, both inside and outside of the hospital, as well as to new clients. In a sense, they have outlived their "creator", which is a good and healthy sign.

CHAPTER VIII
THE PLACE: THE HOSPITAL

> ". . . to bridge the gap between the large state hospitals and the communities they serve."

The hospital makes us think of all the "im-" words which carry so much more absolute negativity than mere negatives: Immovable . . . Impervious . . . Impregnable . . . and . . . Impossible! It really should be called an "imstitution", not a hospital where the sick are supposed to be made well.

The Case Aide Program, was situated in, but was not a part of, the hospital. In order to operate, we had to understand, to whatever degree possible, how the hospital worked and the implications for us of its policies and procedures.

I. THE HOSPITAL STRUCTURE

There were several opposing forces operating at counterpoint to each other. To understand the institution, these forces and the tension between them need to be examined:

A. Departmental vs. Geographical
B. Professional vs. Civil Servant
C. Therapeutic vs. Administrative

There seemed to be constant conflict between these aspects of the hospital's organizational structure.

A. Departmental vs. Geographical

Prior to 1970, the hospital was organized along departmental lines and structural departments had evolved, each responsible for performing one of the hospital's necessary services. For example, there were departments of psychiatry, of social work, nursing, housekeeping, etc. All staff—doctors through janitors—were employed within these departments and were responsible to the departmental director for the performance of their assigned duties. "Who reported to whom" was clearly delineated with each department having its own professional hierarchy.

Each department was responsible for the performance of certain necessary tasks depending upon the particular professional expertise of that department. For example, nurses performed nursing functions, such as dispensing medication, daily ward supervision, and housekeeping performed janitorial duties, such as cleaning. Thus the delineation of "who does what" was fairly well defined. Various special services, such as a separate treatment ward for the care of alcoholics, out-patient care, etc., were performed by various departmental staffs depending upon the service to which they were assigned.

Patients, in this organizational structure, were placed on wards according to two main divisions: acute and chronic. Within this major differentiation, particular wards were organized according to degree of illness with free wards, semi-closed wards, locked wards.

This system, as described, had operated for about 35 years with departments being added as sophistication in patient care and treatment developed over the years.

After 1970, drastic changes were made in the hospital in keeping with new thinking throughout the state. It was thought that the isolated, large state facility was an expensive failure, and that smaller, community based facilities would be more successful and efficient for approaching the problems of mental illness. So, community mental health centers were set up in the various locales with each center mandated to provide in-patient and out-patient care, partial hospital care (such as day care, weekend care, emergency psychiatric care), and consultative and educational services to the general community as a preventive measure.

At this point in time, large institutions were in existence and community centers were in the process of development. What was the interface between these two systems? The statewide plan was that the major responsibility for patient care would be shifted to the community centers as the first line of defense, as it were. For example, the preventive components of the community mental health centers would be catching potential problems at earlier stages, hopefully eliminating the need for long-term hospitalizations. Caught earlier, many "new" patients could be treated with short admissions, partial hospitalizations, or out-patient care—all delivered within the confines of the patient's community, thereby diminishing the admission rate of the state mental hospital. Secondly, for the patients already in the state hospital, every effort should be made to decrease the length of their stay and return them to the community. The hospital was restructured to reflect this change of thinking and philosophy. The geographic area from which the hospital drew its patients was subdivided into three specific community areas—each of which was to have its local mental health center. And, the hospital was subdivided into three main "units" which corresponded to these same areas.

Staff was redistributed out of the old departmental system into the unit system. Each unit had a psychiatrist as director and included other doctors, residents, nurses, social workers, psychologists, attendants, and so on. Each unit had responsibility for delivering hospital services to patients from their particular assigned area. In addition, certain special services were made into separate functional units, not connected to the geographic system, responsible for providing service to the total patient population regardless of geography. Patients were re-assigned onto wards depending on their residence prior to admission, although the chronic and acute differentiation was maintained for management purposes.

If you think it is confusing to read this, it is only because it was truly a complex and confusing process. We will elaborate on some of the effects unitization had on employees, patients, and our particular program.

Staff was confused about who was responsible for what and to whom. For example, if you were a social worker assigned to a geographic unit, who was your boss? Was he the unit director, a psychiatrist, or the director of social service—the department head under the old system who still retained the title? Were you responsible sometimes to one and sometimes to the other, and, if so, over what issues and who decided? Often times, such issues were decided by whoever yelled the loudest, and, at the same time, some staff went into hiding and reported to no one while many were paralyzed by battles over authority with little energy left for patient care. There was tremendous duplication and overlapping of services as well as authority.

The mainstream of hospital life was centered in the geographic units; the special services, such as the Case Aide Program, tended to be either left out of or inundated by geography. For example, a chronic patient, hospitalized for 30 years, and to whom geography was totally irrelevant, "belonged", in reality, to no one. However, should that same patient be fortunate (or unfortunate) enough to get out into the community and need follow-up service, was the community mental health center responsible? Was the out-patient unit of the hospital? Was the staff of the geographic unit? Or all three?

Not only was the in-house organization an administrative nightmare, but so was the relationship between the hospital and the community mental health centers. In theory, the transition from one system to another was sensible; however, in reality, the interim—when one is being phased out and the other phased in—meant that, while patients could be helped to leave the hospital, the local centers were not yet ready to provide the necessary services. Who was to pick up the slack in the meantime?

B. Therapeutic vs. Administrative

This, the second of the major dichotomies inherent in the hospital's structure, related to the tension between the hospital's mandate to help the mentally ill and the administrative necessity to maintain a large institution. These two goals are quite often incompatible, based as they are on different responsibilities and priorities. For example, the feeding of one thousand people three times a day requires queuing up, rigid schedules, and herding. A mental health practitioner might be more concerned about the atmosphere in which the meals are eaten—that it be relaxed, pleasant, leisurely—while those responsible for the efficient management of the institution require that everyone be fed and that the kitchen staff have enough time to clean up and prepare the next meal. To continue with the example, limited funding means starchy meals. Combined with medication and lack of exercise, such a diet helps to create an unhealthy, overweight and lethargic patient population.

Such examples of the conflicting aspects of hospital life go on and on. What to do if your group meeting and shower time are scheduled at the same time? Or, the day your linen is changed is the staff holiday? It should be noted that most often the administrative need takes precedence over the therapeutic aspects of hospital living. It is hard to understand why this is so; perhaps, because like any bureaucracy, the institution attaches to itself a myriad of procedures which, as they become habit-forming and incorporated as a way of life, are no longer noticed by those involved and just passively accepted, like death and taxes.

C. Professional vs. Civil Service

There were three separate and distinct methods of hiring and advancing the various personnel at the hospital: belonging to craft unions, having professional training to be qualified, or being part of the state civil service system. Social workers, for example, were relatively "late-comers" to the hospital scene and were originally covered by civil service. Later, professional educational requirements were superimposed. Thus, some "social workers" held jobs for which they were not qualified because they had had enough time-in-grade to have become permanently employed; newer employees had the required Masters degree but still had to qualify under the Civil Service system or they had absolutely no job security. They could, for example, be "bumped": if another professional with both qualifications wanted that particular slot, the former employee would quickly be outside looking in.

This tension between the two systems occurred with a number of employees and led to abuses that wreaked havoc on staff morale. Those who were not firmly entrenched in the civil service system usually were not around long enough to make an impact on patient care or on their colleagues. These staff members were usually either high or low in the professional hierarchy like psychiatric residents or ward attendants. Their turnover rate was extremely high.

On the other hand, the civil servants were there for "life", so to speak. While such a merit system for public employees might have made sense at one time, it now fosters a mentality that is characterized by paper-pushing, maintaining the status quo at all costs, and a dependence on form or appearance, rather than substance. Looking busy was more important than being busy. At moments of extreme frustration, we felt that patients were necessary to maintain the employment rate of the staff, instead of the reverse.

Establishing and enforcing standards for job performance was next to impossible within this atmosphere. If an employee could not be fired, what motivation did he have to perform well? Staff development programs—like good supervision or in-service training—were virtually non-existent. Without guidance, support, or encouragement, doing a *good* job did not seem, after a while, like a worthwhile activity. Once such apathy sets in, it is difficult to distinguish the staff, in some cases, from the chronic patient population. The apathy takes over making the entire institution immovable—nothing can get done, except the basic necessities that maintain the institution. Statements such as, "It's never been done before", "You can't fight City Hall", "that's the way it is", "What can *we* do?" (accompanied by a hopeless sigh) end all arguments, stifle any creative thought, and squelch any independent action.

In our career as state employees, we were never given a job description, never had a supervisory conference, never had our work critically evaluated; yet we were expected to be responsible for anything that went wrong and any wave that got anyone wet. Nor were we given credit for anything that went "right". Our experience was quite typical. We had our professional experience, each other, and the Case Aides to fall back on, but what about a ward attendant who was responsible for the dirtiest and most unrewarding tasks? What did he have? Or a social worker in the frightening position of doing a job for which he was not qualified? They had no defense so, of course, they did nothing.

II. HOSPITAL POWER

Who or what actually controlled this contradictory system? Like any large structure, the formal organizational chart had little to do with actual power, although it may have been responsible for the setting of policy. Implementation of this policy seemed to be controlled by two factors: longevity and the ability to dispense "goodies".

In our hospital, the most consistent employee group was the nursing staff. They had the largest number relative to other professional groupings, and, because of their size, their turnover rate had the least impact.

Nurses were also in a unique position in the employee hierarchy. Service delivery was based on the medical model: doctor, nurse, attendant; other services were ancillary in this model. The doctor, at the head, was ostensibly in control of patient care. Since our medical staff was largely made up of residents—here today and gone tomorrow—they were largely dependent on the nurse for information. Residents were also quite overburdened by the huge populations in their care so they were also dependent on the ward nurse to filter the load. It was the nurse who determined, to a large extent, who saw the doctor. Thus, she, in practice, decided who got to the source of help. Attendants, the closest to actual patient care, but lowest in the hierarchy, were also dependent on the nurse. Attendants had been placed organizationally as part of the department of nursing. In spite of the new geographical structuring, whatever supervision they did receive came from the nursing staff. Nurses actually controlled the entire service delivery team.

Such control could be good or bad for the patients depending on the personality of the nurses. Miss X, for example, was an extremely dominant person. As long as she was in acknowledged control of one particular geographic unit's operation, she ran an efficient shop. Most decisions on this unit had to be made in staff group meetings to allow the doctors to save face. If Miss X liked a plan, it would be implemented; if she didn't, it would be ignored. The nursing staff was "too busy" or the patient would have a "relapse". Other staff, including the doctors, usually succumbed to such blackmail and rarely made unilateral decisions. As a program, we alternated between loving and hating her (as did the patients) because having her concurrence was like being on the side of the angels, but, without it, we couldn't set foot on one of her wards—no way—no how—even if invited by one of the staff doctors. Actually, she was quite like "Big Nurse" of Ken Kesey's *One Flew Over the Cuckoo's Nest,* whose major weapon was a biting underhanded sarcasm: the "now, we are getting very emotional over this and we don't want to be irrational, do we?" type, when all you want to do is scream, "Yes, I want to be irrational, damn you!" But that only proves her point, "doesn't it, dear?"

Miss Y was different. She has been there as long as Miss X, but handled the control issue differently. Her personality was warm and quite loving. She used her nursing function—touching, healing—as a mother substitute. Her patients were her "babies", her "children", her "chickadees". She wanted to do for them and was marvellously successful. The patients, especially the long term chronic ones, adored her; but, they didn't get well. She could bring back the spark of life, made her patients want to live again, but, unfortunately, only up to a point and then could not let them go, because separation would have been too painful for her.

Then there was Miss Z—young, intelligent, and caring, but caught up in the terrible tragedy of the hospital. She tried to do a job within the aura of hospital abuses. Her staff was apathetic and into sick relationships among each other and with the patients, colored by sex, alcohol, and drugs. Protected by civil service, they were firmly there and without eye-witness testimony, her hands were tied. Who would cast the first stone—a patient, a co-conspirator? So, slowly, Miss Z. became an ostrich and carried on doing what she could, when she could, for as long as she could. Then, she had to choose: stay and become like "them" or get out in spite of her real desire to help the tortured people in her care, both patients and staff.

A different—but equally powerful control—was exercised by the hospital steward who controlled the hospital supplies.

This operational control could shut down an operation, for example, if proper requisitions were not available or the paper supply, from toilet paper to envelopes, was not forthcoming, or the particular telephone budget was needed elsewhere. The steward's power was not very evident in the operation of on-going wards, for instance, but it was absolutely crucial in order to establish or maintain new programs such as the Case Aide unit. The steward reminded us of an old time Irish Democratic ward heeler—colorful, impish, intelligent, and downright dishonest. He was delightful and fun to deal with as long as you held onto your wallet and your virtue. But he, too, was, in a way, a victim of the institutional system. If those who were mandated to exercise responsible control actually performed adequately, his power would have been considerably diminished. When those responsible for good patient care abdicated their positions, someone had to run the institution. The steward just stepped into the power vacuum. However, he saw his job, and justifiably so, as the operation of the institution, not patient treatment. But, as his power and control grew, he got this responsibility as well, since no one else had the guts necessary to make decisions.

III. HOSPITAL PURPOSE

In all this administrative complexity, it was difficult to remember what the hospital was supposed to do, who it was for, and if it was accomplishing its mandated tasks. As with other social problems, the public at large is confused and paradoxical in its thinking about the mentally ill. This confusion is reflected in the hospital. Is it supposed to treat and make well, or only get the mentally ill off the streets and away from us "sane" people? If the hospital's purpose is isolation, why waste millions of dollars on treatment staff? We could use the money to make the isolation facility at least humane. However, if the purpose is rehabilitation, why waste three quarters of your budget on institutional maintenance? Or sacrifice experimentation and creativity because it is too "expensive"?

To make sense of the administrative morass, we need only to decide what it is that we want to do. We do not have to spend more money. For example, those closest to patient care—the attendants—receive the least amount of supervision and training, have the least professional requirements, and are the lowest paid. It would be more rational to reverse the system—scrap the medical model—and build all service delivery around the attendant using the other professionals—nurses, doctors, social workers, etc.—as consultants, supervisors, and trainers who provide the necessary support and back-up.

There was no system of evaluation that we could see whereby a judgment was made whether the hospital was doing what it was "supposed" to be doing. They seemed to judge themselves—like the blind leading the blind—and the criteria used was the number of beds empty or filled. To us, such an indicator signified only the number of beds, not what happened to the people who occupied them. Such a lack of responsible and valid accountability filtered all the way down through the ranks. After the first year of hospitalization, a patient was required to be seen by his doctor only *once a year*; social workers carried case-loads of 125 patients each; nurses spent almost all their time dispensing tons of pills. Hospital accreditation meant a new coat of paint for the wards, not a review of patient care. Community "visiting" committees saw staff, not patients. That anyone got well in such a system seemed a miracle of major proportions.

V. BRIDGING THE GAP BETWEEN HOSPITAL AND COMMUNITY

Originally, the Case Aide Program was conceived as a way to bring together the hospital and the community, two totally different systems, each moving in its own separate spheres. While we tried to bring these two spheres into, at least, touching distance, we were not as successful with this goal as we were with the others.

There was no known model on which to pattern an operation totally in the interface between two systems. Several alternatives were tried. One of these was community-based Case Aide programs located in the community mental health centers. However, as soon as these were operational, they immediately moved into prevention areas—the primary goal of the mental health center—and had little left over for after-care which was the purpose that we had in mind. Then the problems of territory—or overlapping responsibility—became overwhelming. Did we pick up when a community patient was hospitalized or did they keep the community Case Aide? Who provided supervision and/or backup for the patient/case aide relationship as the pair moved out of the hospital—us or the community program?

As the patient moved into the community we had to make decisions about priorities. While in the hospital, the Case Aide relationship was a powerful sustaining force. Outside, however, other problems became tantamount, such as the absolute lack of living facilities other than boarding houses or nursing homes, the only available alternatives. As a program, we had to begin dealing directly with these issues.

We had begun to consider sacrificing some treatment relationships in order to devote more time and energy to resolving bread and butter issues such as developing cooperative apartments, half way houses, and recreational programs, to name a few, but as already described, fate intervened. Unfortunately, it intervened at a time when a "community connection" was becoming absolutely essential as the state-wide mental health dictum to move out patients into the community was acclerated.

CHAPTER IX
THE END: A PROGRAM IN RETROSPECT

What made this volunteer program different from others? What made the Case Aide Program demonstrably effective over a long period of time? There are definite components that we believe contributed to its success:

1. *Purpose:* Case Aides were more than casual friendly visitors. They visited for an explicitly therapeutic purpose and with a clearly delineated plan.

2. *Contract:* All participants knew what they were there for and for how long.

3. *Back-up:* Case Aide/Patient relationships were supported by professional supervision and training. Perhaps, more important than the professional aspects of the back-up available to Case Aides were the emotional supports that were given. Since they were not being paid, we wanted to give to them in other ways—our time, our skills, and ourselves. We had to be *there.*

4. *Identity:* They were not "just" volunteers; they had a name to be proud of, a special identity, and a positive philosophy that helped to give prestige and substance to their contribution.

5. *Responsibility:* The Case Aide was expected to be the coordinator of all aspects of the patient's treatment course. It was the Case Aide's responsibility to see that everything that

needed to be done did actually get done no matter who he had to "take on" to accomplish this task, whether this be the Case Aide supervisors themselves, hospital staff, community caretakers, etc.

Difficult and incomplete as it may be, we have tried to define the Case Aide Program as a workable model for effective service delivery. The use of volunteer paraprofessionals as treatment deliverers or change agents is a good way to accomplish a great deal economically and efficiently. To us, who have experienced such a method, it seems a sensible way to operate. Why, however, are volunteer paraprofessionals so under-utilized? We have heard reasons such as the following:

"They can't do what professionals can." Why not, if they have professional back-up? Or, do we really want them to do what professionals do? We can choose either alternative according to their skills and our goals.

"Can they be expected to uphold the principles of treatment, i.e. confidentiality, self-determination, etc?" Some can and some cannot, but that is why there is professional screening and supervision.

"It's hard to get and to keep volunteers." We feel that this reasoning is unfounded. If all components "click"—your program meets the needs of the volunteers and the volunteer serves the needs of your program—you can get and keep volunteers. We had a waiting list of people who were eager to volunteer to work in a miserable place with "crazy" people.

"Clients wouldn't want 'just a volunteer' ". Such resistance is quickly and easily overcome by a sincere and responsible individual who is part of a program that is truly responsive to the needs of its clients.

"If a volunteer paraprofessional is used, what happens to the professional?" This is a good point, and perhaps one of the more important reasons for the paucity of such programs. This argument has a certain amount of substance. We, as social workers, for example, are caught in a bind; great need, little money, fewer paid positions, greater competition, and irrelevant training. The issue here is really concerned with the future of professionals as such. Whether or not paraprofessionals are on the scene is not germane to the central issue of the future of paid service deliverers.

SERVICE GAPS

While we cannot address ourselves to all trends and issues, we did become involved in one specific issue that most directly touched upon our program:

> the shift from isolated institutions to small community agencies and the service gaps therein.

We all know that there are many people who will be leaving hospitals and special schools for the handicapped throughout the country. In theory, most of us will probably agree that it is a good thing to close these miserable facilities and shift the responsibility and programming back to the community. But, realistically, there are tremendous gaps; these former patients and inmates are not being prepared for this dramatic change from institution to "every day" living. The public seems not to be ready for these "different" people and is often fearful and resentful of these "kooks" from the asylums. And, the very agencies that are being funded and staffed to deal with this population are equally unprepared to cope with people who have been institutionalized. Their first responsibility is to serve the population already in their community, so out come numbers of frightened people with no place to go, and no one that has been delegated or designated to help with this transitional step.

One of the most prominent of these gaps is that of aftercare; who is responsible for the person who has left the hospital? Is it the hospital staff? Or is it the community mental health center? Or is it both? Invariably, when John Jones left the hospital, he was given enough medication for a month, some advice, and was usually told that he could come back for one or two visits if needed. The real problems usually arose months later when he had been out for a few months and the euphoria wore off. He may have lost his job, had another fight with his parents or wife, or stopped taking his medication. Now, whom should he call? He usually called his Case Aide, who then tried to make an appointment with a local doctor or a psychiatrist from the community mental health facility. Very often, these doctors had waiting lists, or were too expensive, or else felt that they did not know the patient well enough, and so recommended his "state" doctor, who was totally overwhelmed with his large numbers of in-patients. The patient and his family often became the ping-pong ball batted between the two service systems as they argued about who was responsible or "busier".

The problem of after care is of substantial proportions. Statistics have often been reported that as many as 70% of the admissions to the hospital we were working in were, in actuality, re-admissions. The revolving door effect must be addressed and seems to be directly related to the needs and placehent of staff, not patients. The staff was in the hospital, therefore they could only deal with in-house situations. They were not equipped to deal in the community. On the other hand, the community caretakers were not equipped to deal in the residual effects of "hospitalism". The patient was caught in the middle.

To compound this problem of after care is the problem of family involvement; many people who have been hospitalized for a long time have no family to return to, or anyone who will be available to them when they leave the hospital. There are numerous reasons for the isolation of the mentally ill. Family members also might have suffered from the patient's illness and just could not or would not try again, or family members who tried to remain involved were often turned off by the hospital staff who excluded them from the patient's treatment. More often than not, the years and physical distance were the essential variables that separated families. Regardless of the reasons, the results were the same, so that we were generally dealing with people who had no one. The Case Aide became friend, family, and link to the world outside the hospital. This role was a heavy one for us and for the individual Case Aides as well. Although we could technically set a time limit on the Program's relationship to the individual patient or group, it was difficult to ignore a phone call from Mary when she needed help, even if we had "closed" her case three years before. Many of the Case Aides generously continued to keep in touch with their clients for years; they sometimes called their former supervisors for advice. None of us could say "no" when we felt that we might be the only shield between that individual and re-hospitalization. We made every effort, during the Case Aide year, to connect people with community resources, but it is hard to anticipate the crises that so often occur and with which these emotionally "fragile" people are often less equipped to deal. Also, the resources were usually just not there.

Frequently, then, we saw people being dumped into nursing homes and into lonely, cheap rooms in delapidated boarding houses and hotels. The rationale of the hospital staff was that they had to reduce the hospital census figures and that the patients were really better off out there anyway. This was a difficult statement to dispute, since we too often shared this goal, but our approach was quite different. We offered a relationship, a plan, and a sharing and caring involvement. We did not put people anywhere; it was a mutually decided and thoughtfully worked out decision. Follow-up was an integral part of the plan, and if a person was unhappy with a family care home, his room, or whatever arrangement that had been made, we helped him to either resolve the difficulties or to find a more satisfactory situation. We did not see the placement as final and irrevocable, but as a part of a normal growth and development process.

There are very few state-supported half-way houses for the adult mentally ill; there were none at all at this particular hospital and only a dozen in the entire state. There must be a variety of possibilities since there are such a variety of individual needs. There is a need for housing for the older, more chronic individual as well as the young working person; there is a need for temporary or transitional residents. The big problem in this area is that no one knows who is responsible for establishing them, nor is there a clear mechanism for their funding. We found that such jurisdictional problems could be sidestepped by helping patients to develop private living situations of their own. Because these small scale cooperative apartments were self-initiated and self-supported, they were therefore more normal than a labelled "patient" facility. These apartments are possibilities even for those patients who can not sustain employment, since many do qualify for benefits such as Social Security or Welfare assistance.

Another area of great need was that of socialization. It was so difficult for people who had been hospitalized to risk themselves in new relationships and in new situations. So often, we saw people just getting stuck. They were forced to depend on the good will of Case Aides, past and present, and the uneven services of community agencies. Most of these agencies only intervened if the person became overtly ill; they were lax in providing supportive services to this population on an on-going basis. Often, then, the only way that a recently discharged person could qualify for service was to become "crazy" again.

IMPLICATIONS AND APPLICATIONS

Now, we have a program model and we also have glaring needs. We did not have time, in our particular operation, to really develop other programs that we felt could have brought the prototype and the gaps together.

We wanted to establish a smooth flow of Case Aide service from inside the hospital to the outside and from that limbo of just being outside to being a real part of the community; we had accomplished the first part of this agenda. The second half was trickier, but we had begun to move in these directions. Efforts to coordinate and to link up existing services were abortive; we had begun to realize that we would have to bring the Case Aide idea physically out into the community as an adjunct to the services provided within the hospital.

We are no longer in the position to do it ourselves; yet our thoughts and plans might help others to implement such projects. We see "case aides" as having the skills and expertise to man programs in the following areas:

1. *After-Care Programs* whose impetus would come mainly from the hospitals to which the patient is often still emotionally tied. The emphasis, in the beginning, would be the introduction to basic living skills and then a gradual shift to community integration.
2. *"After-After"-Care Programs* would be the next step, since the second adjustment that a patient must make—outside the hospital but not yet "in" the community—is as great, in reality, as the first step out. This is where most aftercare programs fall apart. How does an ex-patient get into the social network? There is a need for a community-based Case Aide relationship during this phase—someone who can invite the patient to church, introduce him to neighbors, or just go to a movie.

3. *Socialization Programs* where the community residents and the hospitalized patient share common experiences before discharge, such as integrated religious services, voter registration drives, co-sponsoring of cultural events.
4. *Housing Programs* could begin in the hospitals if wards could be changed to apartments with the emotional and financial resources of Case Aides. In addition, Case Aides could be developers of housing facilities, because who are better equipped than community residents to know where and how? Such programs need to be related to specific patients; general committees, we have found, get bogged down in administrative red tape and "studies".
5. *Community Education* could be provided by Case Aide consultants who are familiar both with the problems of the institutionalized individual and the concerns of the community resident.

The use of volunteers raises some ethical issues both on the current operation of existing social agencies and in social work education. The dearth of relevant uses of volunteer skills is due, not to the volunteers themselves, but to the professionals who, for the most part, are not equipped or willing to deal with them. There are two factors involved:

1. lack of appreciation and respect for the skills and talents of the non-professional;
2. fear of being replaced, of losing prestige.

We believe that the professional schools providing training for the human services could provide more relevant curricula. Professionals, in our judgment, do not know how or where to use adjunctive personnel. We no longer need "more" people doing the same things that they have always done, i.e. direct service work. Instead, we need to develop new roles for the professionals, especially social workers, which is our particular expertise, in the following areas: program planning, administration, interdisciplinary collaboration, human resource consultation, program research and evaluation, and the development of training and educational possibilities.

Specifically, we are advocating the use of volunteers as a manpower resource. In order to capitalize on this potential, the schools must begin to train degree candidates to do what is needed, not what the schools feel they should know. For example, "new" professionals, right out of school, should have some experience in supervision, program administration, and the evaluation of their own practice. In addition, relevant continuing education programs are needed for us "oldies" whose skills may be becoming obsolete.

We have written this book because we continue to be haunted by the unfulfilled needs of one population—the mentally ill. We are sure that there are others just as needy, just as forgotten, and just as accessible to this model of intervention that we used in the Case Aide Program. In our mind's eye, there is the constant picture of a darkened and barren hall filled with hopeless, shuffling people . . . waiting . . .

THE CASE AIDE HANDBOOK

A Creative Role For The Volunteer

By
Barbara Baroff Feinstein
and
Catherine Catterson Cavanaugh

THE CASE AIDE PROGRAM

A Creative Role For the Volunteer

Authors

Barbara Baroff Feinstein, M.S.W., A.C.S.W.
Catherine Catterson Cavanaugh, M.S.W., C.S.W.

APPENDIX A

Acknowledgments

We dedicate this manual to the many who have said to us; "The Case Aides and the Case Aide Program changed my life; I hope there will be more programs like this for other people."

The authors gratefully acknowledge the experience and support of all the Case Aides; without their concern, energy and encouragement, we might not have written this manual. Certainly, the patients have been our inspiration also.

Introduction

During its seven year history, the Case Aide Program has grown tremendously. Beginning with one part-time professional and 12 volunteers, the program has brought, to date, more than 300 volunteer Case Aides to the hospital donating their time, their enthusiasm, and their concern for their fellow man to over 300 patients. About 20% of these volunteers have gone on to careers in the mental health professions.

Who is the Case Aide? The Case Aide is an interested and concerned community resident, who may have little or no professional training in the field of mental health, but who has a sincere desire to be helpful to another human being and is willing to make a commitment of three hours a week for one year.

We have been receiving numerous requests for information about the training and use of the paraprofessional. This manual is an attempt to respond—an attempt to put on paper what we have learned from working with these special people—the Case Aides.

We must describe our own program—its goals and philosophy, its structure, and its relationship to the host agency—in order to extract the more general principles pertinent to any volunteer program.

THE CASE AIDE PROGRAM

I. Purpose, Goals, and Philosophy

A. *Purpose.* Having identified our purpose, the resocialization of the long term chronic mental patient, the next step was the determination of the most viable vehicle with which to meet this need. It was felt that goal-oriented, person-to-person contact would be most compatible with the purpose, goals and philosophy that had been developed.

B. *Goals.* The goals of this program are fourfold:

1. to help resocialize a mental patient so that he or she may become a useful citizen capable of making a life with dignity and pride;

2. to provide community residents with an opportunity to learn new skills and make a meaningful contribution to the life of their community;

3. to bridge the gap between the mental health service delivery system of the state hospital and the communities which it serves;

4. to extend the treatment reach of the social worker through the use of competent paraprofessionals.

These goals could be easily generalized to pertain to various settings and populations. For example, a chronic disease hospital has a different population from ours, but with very similar needs and problems. It is easy to envision the adoption of all of the goals outlined with minor modifications. Another application of these goals is in family service: volunteer units could be beneficial to the elderly, the multi-problem family, and to other isolated groups.

The fact that our program is staffed by two professional social workers gives the program the special characteristics of this field: individual supervision, goal-oriented casework, and community resource utilization. Obviously, if such a program were administered by other professional or non-professional groups, there would be a different flavor to the actual delivery of the service. For example, should the supervisor be a psychiatric nurse, the emphasis might be more on medical and/or physical care of the consumer.

C. *Philosophy*. As described, the social work orientation also influences the philosophy of the program. The role of the Case Aide is based on three fundamental principles:

1. Relationship: The Case Aide Program is based on the philosophy that a firm relationship with an individual who really cares is the basis of all change. Friendliness, respect for the rights of each individual, attention to the small details that no one else may have time for, consistency, and the recognition of the dignity of each of our patients are the atmosphere that we try to foster at all times. It is in this milieu that patients begin to experience themselves as worthwhile, important men and women.

2. Helping: The job of the Case Aide is *to help, not to treat*. We deal with the present, the rational, and the healthy behavior of our patients. Our orientation seeks to ask what we can accomplish right now, today, that will help the situation. The spontaneous emotional response of the Case Aide, under supervision, is the motivating and engaging force vis à vis the patient. The Case Aide will try to help the patient obtain what he needs to accomplish the agreed-upon goals. These needs may be financial support, new glasses, transportation to and from a job, a room, a foster family, more adequate clothing, social skills, learning to read and write. Case Aides will pull together the resources of the hospital, the community, and their own creative talents—as well as those of the patients—to accomplish the goals.

3. *Dehospitalization*. The thinking behind the program is that some patients, especially chronic, long-term hospitalized patients, need to be reoriented to the world outside the hospital grounds. The Case Aide, having no official status in the hospital hierarchy, has been described as "fresh air" by the patients. A major goal of the relationship is to point the patient away from the hospital and toward the community.

Meetings on the wards between patient and Case Aide are discouraged. The pairs meet initially in the Case Aide office area, where pleasant, colorful meeting rooms are available and coffee is always hot.

The office is located on the top floor of the main, old "chronic" building where the majority of the patients are housed. With the help of the Case Aides and of other friends of the program, we have decorated and furnished what was originally a drab ward area.

If feasible, Case Aides and patients make full use of the restaurants, social and recreational activities, shopping centers, transportation, etc., in the surrounding communities.

D. *Atmosphere.* A feeling of warmth, concern, and purpose pervades the program providing a special, somewhat indefinable, quality which is the heart of the program. It is this atmosphere which:

—shapes the meaning behind all the techniques, theories, and planning;

—gives the Case Aide a sense of belonging, of being effective, of doing something worthwhile, of making a difference;

—gives the patient a sense of being special, of counting, of being hopeful;

—gives the professional an appreciation of the value of people-to-people experience, and of the joy of being part of such positive relationships.

How is this positive atmosphere created? A basic ingredient is the personal attitude of the supervisors toward the paraprofessionals, the patients, and the helping process. If you value the contribution that volunteers can make, you will free them to be effective as helpers and to develop as human beings. Beyond the intangible elements of the "atmosphere", it is important to recognize that the physical plant must reflect the same philosophy. Cheerfully painted walls, "homey" furniture, unlocked doors, private bathroom facilities, the smell of fresh coffee, all make their contribution.

II. The Case Aide

Any program stands or falls on the quality of the personnel who are called upon to implement the service. In our case, these people are the Case Aides. Our volunteers range in age from 20 to 70. They come from many of the communities that the hospital serves, bringing formal education or the experience of life. They are housewives, retired corporation executives, nurses, secretaries, engineers, teachers, and college students. Many are exploring avenues for their future careers in the mental health professions; some are reorganizing their life styles as they are approaching middle age; others are "keeping their hand in" while raising their families; all are interested in being helpful to another person. A full complement of Case Aides in one year is 65.

Perhaps it would be helpful to describe several Case Aides, to illustrate some of the diversity and commonality among these volunteers.

Mrs. A. is a forty-five year old housewife with a husband and three teenage children. She is a high school graduate, and over the years has taken adult education courses ranging from pottery to psychology. Always involved in civic activities, whether it be church or school, Mrs. A. has no career aspirations; her major motivation is to help another human being.

Mrs. B. is a thirty-two year old college graduate, who has a young family and has not been in the work arena since her children were born. She is beginning to think about her own professional career; she is career-testing. Mrs. B. may have had some work or academic experience in the mental health field prior to her marriage.

Mr. C. is a retired businessman who for the first time in years has the opportunity to pursue, in a volunteer capacity, a field in which he has long been interested. He brings a very special dimension to his Case Aide work, a strong practical and business orientation, as well as a personal freedom from job or family pressures.

Miss D. is a senior in college and is utilizing her Case Aide experience for a practicum in social work. Although she has had many psychology and sociology courses, she has not had direct clinical experience and she is anxious to find out if she can be helpful to people, and also if she will like and be suitable for this field.

Mr. E., a young man in his thirties, is a very successful engineer; he feels that his job situation is not fulfilling—that something is "missing." This program is an opportunity for him to express other qualities such as sensitivity, warmth, and caring.

A. *Recruitment.* In order to publicize the program and attract new volunteers, we must use all the resources of the media to which we have access:

1. Letters to local newspapers, as well as feature articles;
2. public service announcements on radio and television;
3. guest spots and news features on major television and radio networks, in addition to programming on the educational channels.

Most important in attracting qualified people is the personal salesmanship of the Case Aides themselves and others who have had contact with the program.

We have found that our own participation in the organizational life of the communities that the hospital serves is another way of publicizing the program and of keeping it responsive. Some of the methods we have used are: appearing on panel discussions, speaking engagements at church and community groups, and liaison work with mental health agencies.

We also make a special effort to work with organizations that are attempting to raise the social awareness of their memberships. Groups such as the mental health associations, League of Women Voters, the

National Organization for Women, and local community colleges, have a natural affinity for programs such as ours, since it can provide opportunities for training and career testing.

The psychology, sociology, and counselling departments of the colleges in the area are also attracted to the Case Aide Program because it can provide undergraduates and graduate students with a relevant field practice experience.

B. *Screening.* All of our potential applicants are screened in a personal interview; we also require character references.

One of the first questions we are asked about the program is: "What do you look for in a potential Case Aide?"

1. First impressions count: Does the person's appearance reflect a positive self-image? How does he handle the initial few minutes of the interview? We want someone who has a positive outlook about himself and others and who is able to cope with his own anxieties in an open manner. For example, the person who walks into the office complaining about the directions given and making other negative comments is less likely to succeed than the person who comes in smiling and, though nervous, is able to say, "I hope I can be helpful to people in the hospital."

2. Certain qualities count: We have found our volunteers need the "3 R's"—*Reality, Relating,* and *Resourcefulness.* By reality we mean a large dose of common sense, an ability to maintain perspective and proportion, and a capacity to "see it as it is" while keeping a sense of humor. When we talk about "relating", we are saying that we expect a Case Aide to care enough to respect the patient's right to grow in his own way and to have friendliness that does not smother. Resourcefulness encompasses the ability to put it all together—hospital facilities, supervision, community, and self *on behalf of the patient.*

3. Motivation counts: An important factor to consider in evaluating Case Aides is "What are they looking for in this program?" We have found that there are three categories of people who do not make effective Case Aides and we try to screen them out. The first category may be described as the "super-intellectualizers", they want to meet a "catatonic schizophrenic". The second is "Mrs. Goody-Two-Shoes". She wants to help those "poor people". And the third category want to get vicarious therapy for their own personal problems.

Briefly, the successful Case Aides are those who can give more than they get.

For those Case Aides who seek to use the program as a practicum for a university course, we desire close coordination of our program with the course content. Since our program is located in an unused chronic hospital ward, the screening interview serves as an initial introduction to the state hospital setting. We invite potential candidates, whenever possible, to attend one of our training seminars so that they can get a feel for the program, in order to decide more realistically if this experience is what they want.[1]

C. *Commitment.* To insure quality service for the patients and, at the same time, to provide a sense of purpose for the Case Aides, we ask that potential Case Aides make certain commitments to the program:

1. They must remain in the program at least one year.
2. They must see their assigned patients once a week, preferably on the same day each week, for one hour.
3. They must submit weekly written reports and statistics on their contacts with their patients and on their feelings about the contacts. These reports are the basis for diagnostic evaluation and treatment planning. They are also useful in assessing the potential and present skills of the particular volunteer.
4. They must attend weekly training seminars with other Case Aides.

The majority of our patients come to us through referral from the hospital staff, who are responsible for the initial screening of patients and for bringing to our attention those people who could most benefit from our services. However, we do also consider patients who refer themselves or are brought in by their friends. The form[2] that we have developed to aid staff in their referring process has another purpose, which is the immediate and continuing commitment of that staff person.

The Case Aide Program itself then interviews each patient prior to acceptance.[3] There are some very basic criteria that must be met by each patient referred. It is necessary that a potential user of Case Aide services be moderately verbal, in some degree of contact with reality, have some thoughts about future plans, and choose to participate in the program.

We have worked with a very diverse population of all ages and a wide range of diagnoses. The majority of our caseload have been the more stable, chronically hospitalized patients who seem able to benefit from the fruits of a long-term relationship. We also have worked with the acutely ill person who needs a short-term, specific service involving the Case Aide in family, community, and service systems. The Case Aides have also been involved with patients referred directly from aftercare facilities in the community. There is still a difficulty in

1. See Screening Form for Case Aides in Appendix A.
2. See referral form for patients in Appendix A.
3. See patient card in Appendix A.

working out relationships between the in-patients and the aftercare follow-up services.

We have discussed the formation of the Case Aide Program and how we recruit the Case Aides. The next section will describe how these two components of the service system are combined to implement the program.

III. The Organization and Structure of the Program

The core of the Case Aide Program is the relationship that is established between the Case Aide and the patient to whom he is assigned. After the initial screening and acceptance of the Case Aide, the supervisors match the volunteer to a patient who has been accepted by the program.

A. *Matching.* Matching the patient to the Case Aide is a complicated task; the criteria used vary from situation to situation. Factors taken into account include the background of both patient and volunteer, special interests of each, personality characteristics, educational level and the treatment program initially decided upon. Some matches are quite conventional:

—a 40 year old male self-employed engineer to a patient in his late 20's with an engineering background, but with extremely low self-esteem and fears about leaving the protection of the hospital.

—a middle-aged attractive divorcee to a woman patient of comparable age who could not adjust to separation from her parents, who never married, denied her femininity, and turned for solace to alcohol.

—a young housewife with three small children living in an isolated suburb to a young housewife living in almost identical circumstances, but feeling overwhelmed by her family responsibilities.

In other situations, we have tried different combinations with sometimes magical results:

—a female college student with an exceptionally mature and accepting manner to an older man who was unable to find a place in the world after fighting in World War II, rootless, without family, with a long history of negativism, hopelessness, and alcoholism.

—a college student who looked much younger than her 21 years to a woman with a 20-year history of severe marital difficulties and an inability to relate successfully to her five children.

B. *Timing.* We usually begin all our new Case Aides in the early Fall. All Case Aides are assigned to their patients and their training groups during one week. Since all Case Aides, at this point, are in a similar position, orientation, as well as Case Aide group identification, are facilitated.

The Case Aide is given only essential identifying data about his patient before the initial introduction. A meeting between the two is arranged before the Case Aide begins training. We feel strongly that the first impressions gained in this manner are more helpful since they are not colored by diagnostic material or the opinions of staff members. This initial meeting also tends to allay the anxieties of both the Case Aide and the patient because the largest step has been taken. The Case Aide is now involved. We feel that the training seminars are more relevant to the needs of the Case Aide, and indirectly to his patient, when the Case Aide is already working with him and thinking in terms of what he can do or say. The anxiety of beginning is immediately channeled into constructive activity. After this first meeting with his patient, the Case Aide returns to the office area for his first training seminar.

Consultation with concerned staff members and use of the case records can be arranged for the Case Aide through the supervisors early in the year and when appropriate or needed thereafter.

C. *The Case Aide Training Group.* We try to match patients with volunteers who come from the same community. We also assign Case Aides to training groups which are organized on the same geographic lines.

The training group is the vehicle that the supervisors use to impart specific information that the Case Aides must know about the hospital—rules, staff, organization, etc. The group also provides a forum for the discussion of mental health principles. Topics such as the elements of establishing a relationship, interviewing skills, diagnostic classifications and what they mean, family dynamics, etc. are discussed.

The Case Aides can also use the group for mutual support and encouragement. They are encouraged to express their own feelings about what they are doing and are encouraged to take more and more responsibility about their own learning as they become familiar with the program, their patient's needs, and their own attitudes and goals.

Supervision is done in this group atmosphere, as well as individual conferences. The sharing of particular questions and concerns fosters the supportive function of the group. Helping each other with comments and suggestions is also a valuable learning experience.

D. *Seminar Content.* We now have our Case Aides matched to their patients and assigned to a training group of about 10-12 members. What do we do now?

Based on our experience, we have found that the year's program is divided into three parts: orientation, implementation, and termination.

1. *Orientation.* The Case Aide needs to become familiar with the hospital, its staff, and its structure. They also need to begin to know and to relate to one another and to the supervisors. And equally im-

portant, it is necessary for the Case Aide to talk about his initial experiences and impressions.

It is in this stage that the meeting needs to be most carefully structured. The Case Aide's anxiety is extremely high and his only support at this point comes from the group. Therefore, patient interviewing time, group hours, and conference schedules are firmly maintained. We introduce weekly written reports[4] and statistics[5] immediately. Technical material has proven helpful and reassuring at this point. We have gathered together much of this material into a *Case Aide Handbook* which is the basis for our initial discussions. It contains topics such as:

Objectives of the Program
Who is the Case Aide?
Responsibilities of a Case Aide: "The Contract"
Some Rules of Thumb: "Do's and Don'ts"
Relationship
Interviewing
Medication
Classification of Mental Illness
Steps in Readiness to Leave
Unitization
Hospital Procedures
Commitment Laws
Hospital Facilities
Reading of Interest
Map of Hospital

We feel it is important for all volunteers to have this type of guide. The material is covered in about four months. Within this period, there is variation within each training group reflective of the group composition. For example, some groups prefer focusing on the patients and on theories and intellectual discussion, while other groups seem more concerned about their own personal reactions to their patients and to relationships. These differences indicate to us the type of techniques that we would use in teaching the individual seminar group. We relate to each group where they are. For example, the more "intellectual" group responds better to formal lectures, review of the literature, "professional" guest speakers, etc., whereas "the relaters" are more comfortable with informal case reviews with their fellow Case Aides, movies, low-keyed group supervision, and resource oriented guest speakers.

4. See patient interview summation in Appendix A.
5. See Appendix B.

Obviously, it is difficult to always have such homogeneous training groups. Yet, our experience has proven that there is usually a dominant faction in the group, although we certainly respect and respond to the needs of the minority. It should be remembered that the training seminar is always supplemented by individual supervision.

By this time, the group itself has evolved an identity with the program and with each other. They have also become more familiar with their facility, and they have established a relationship with their patients. It is important to note that if the Case Aide has not accomplished all three tasks, but most especially the relationship with the patient, the contract with the program will probably be broken. If the Case Aide does not develop this sense of commitment, he is not involved enough to persevere in a difficult, demanding, and somewhat unrewarding role as a volunteer. As one Case Aide put it, "We're low man on the professional totem pole."

2. *Implementation.* We have evaluated the particular group and its needs; each Case Aide is committed. Now we can really go to work on behalf of the patient. The focus of the supervisors shifts from the Case Aide to the patient. In individual supervision, we can clarify psychosocial diagnoses and treatment plans. In the groups, we move from establishing a relationship to using the relationship. This process is expedited within the groups by frequent case presentations, as well as by constant evaluation of treatment goals. We also encourage patient-focused "putting-together" sessions, such as "How do we handle the family who sabotages?", "How to get John's teeth fixed so he can look for a job?", "What is a good way to approach Dr. Jones?", etc. The Case Aide has grown beyond a friend/relator to an ombudsman.

As part of the new focus, the supervisors try to reflect some of the commonality among diverse patient situations. For example, one Case Aide group might have several patients with problem family involvements. Thus we would organize a series of meetings around topics like family dynamics, family therapy, family service resources. These might be presented by ourselves and/or by pertinent guest speakers. Another area of focus might be community mental health (or the lack thereof) including problems of alternative living situations, job opportunities, follow-up services and aftercare services. An entirely different theme would be in-hospital situations. For instance, the hospital's internal power structure and how to deal with it, the integration of the Case Aide into the particular hospital treatment team, etc. would be possible topics.

The implementation period is the real heart of the training program because this is where the volunteer "makes it happen". The supervisors must maintain a great deal of flexibility during this period, as contrasted to the more structured orientation phase, in responding to both the group needs and the individual patient needs. Although it is helpful to the supervisors to formulate a monthly plan for each of the different Case Aide training groups, they must be prepared to dispense with their agenda on short notice. Obviously, if we are planning to discuss the implication of behavior modification and a Case Aide arrives, upset, saying that the hospital plans an immediate discharge of "John", we could not possibly continue with the planned agenda. We must respond immediately because we know that his family does not want him back, and he has no financial support. What's to be done? As a group, we try to evolve some concrete, workable suggestions and plans.

3. *Termination*. There are two kinds of termination that must be dealt with: that of the patient and that of the Case Aide. These may coincide, or they may not. To reiterate, the Case Aide's contract is for one year. This time frame is clearly understood by the Case Aide and the patient.

Since the goal of the program is to dehospitalize the patient, we use this year as the frame of reference in which to accomplish this task. The majority of the Case Aide/patient pairs do work out this way. Thus we can concentrate our efforts during the last several months on helping both to work through the separation process. The termination is one of the most difficult and complicated aspects of our program, as it is in any therapeutic relationship.

For the most part, the patient is out—is beginning a new life—and thus no longer needs the Case Aide in the same way. The gradual separation process is often a relief to the patient who has begun to develop more independent modes of functioning. The Case Aide should also be able to let go at this point. The Case Aide group meetings are used as a decompression chamber for emotions like loss, anger, guilt, relief, and they are used to generalize the experience and make it an opportunity for personal growth.

On the other hand, there are situations that are not as "neat". The Case Aide may have to leave the program precipitously due to illness or other major life changes. Or the patient may not be ready for the big step outside the hospital after the end of the first year. Then, it becomes the responsibility of the supervisor to review the case and decide what alternatives would be most useful. Do we assign a Case Aide for another year, or do we use the information gleaned already to make recommendations to the staff person who had originally referred the patient?

We have found it helpful to emphasize the over-all relationship of both the Case Aide and the patient to the program in the initial contract. We also achieve such an effect via the availability and back-up of the supervisors. We think it important to meet each patient and to plan joint interviews periodically; this fosters a familiarity with the program on the part of the patient over and above his relationship with a particular Case Aide. Then, if the Case Aide must drop out, the patient still has a sense of contact with the program which can support him until we can make a decision about reassignment.

E. *Individual Supervision.* Each Case Aide relates to a particular supervisor, one of the two psychiatric social workers assigned to the program, for individual help in setting realistic goals with his patient. This strong case-work back-up is an integral part of the work of the program. We have found that concrete, reality-based supervision is more effective than more analytical, intellectual supervision.

Individual conferences are held weekly, bi-monthly, or monthly, depending on the needs of the patient, the comfort and skill of the Case Aide, and the length of time that the relationship has had to develop. The social workers are there also on an as-needed basis for crisis intervention.

F. *Case Aide Development.* We have tried to build into the program a skill development component based on the interests, talent, and potential of the Case Aides. As stated above, the core of the program is the one-to-one relationship. Case Aides entering the program are all exposed to this modality.

Yet, to keep the program meaningful to the volunteers and responsive to emerging needs of the patient population, Case Aides who elect to stay with us more than one year may elect to join a Senior Case Aide group. These Case Aides have demonstrated a high degree of ability to establish and to use themselves effectively within a relationship, a constructive and intelligent use of supervision, and a desire to learn better helping skills.

It is important, in any viable volunteer program, that the individual donating his time and energy be given every opportunity to grow. Rather than keeping each person in a "Case Aide" mold, we try to give him an opportunity to use particular talents and skills in new and creative ways. For example, those with artistic skills do a form of art therapy, and those with writing skills help with the *Case Aide Chronicle*, our program's newspaper.

In addition, we try to enhance the treatment skills of the Case Aides. For example, some Case Aides are asked to be responsible for approximately three or more patients. Such a geometric progression is even more effective in extending the social worker's reach than the series of one-to-one relationships. In this Senior Case Aide group, each member is involved in a project that has been developed to maximize individual interests and skills. Supervision and consultation are provided by the program supervisors. Some examples are:

—teams of two or three Case Aides meet with groups of eight to fifteen patients from one ward around some common theme which may be the development of social interaction skills, the process of finding a job, etc.

—a Case Aide and a unit social worker have been co-leading a group of six women with the specific goal of enabling them to establish an independent living situation. Families of these patients no longer can be involved; therefore, we are trying to create a similar feeling of support and mutual help among the women themselves. We are developing a new approach to alternative living—cooperative apartment sharing with the back-up of the hospital services, the Case Aide, and the community.

—another example of Case Aides as innovators is the Aftercare/Resocializiation Group being established by two Case Aides with the consultation of the supervisors of the Case Aide Program. This group will be available to people who have been hospitalized but are now living at home; many men and women who have been "away" from the normal community life find it difficult to make friends or to develop their social life, so such a group opportunity should be useful and supportive.

IV. Conclusion

In concluding this manual, we would like to re-affirm our tremendous respect for the Case Aides. It is our feeling that there is a vast, almost untapped resource available in the volunteer; it needs only to be channeled. It is our hope that this paper will make a contribution to the utilization of these helpers by delineating the procedures and techniques that we used to create a highly effective treatment program with one neglected population.

APPENDIX A

1. Screening Form for Case Aides (5 x 8 Card)

CASE AIDE

NAME .... SPOUSE .... DATE ....
ADDRESS .... PHONE .... DATE OF BIRTH ....
FAMILY STRUCTURE ....
REASON FOR ENTERING PROGRAM ....
PREVIOUS EDUCATION, JOB OR VOLUNTEER EXPERIENCE
....
SPECIAL INTERESTS ....
PLANS FOR VOCATION OR CAREER ....
REFERENCES: 1 .... 2 ....
....
ACCEPTED .... DATE .... NOT ACCEPTED .... REASON ....

C.A.—reverse

IMPRESSION AT TIME OF INTERVIEW ....
.... SEEN BY ....
SUPERVISOR .... PATIENT 1 .... DATE ....
CONFERENCE SCHEDULE .... 2 .... DATE ....
.... 3 .... DATE ....
COMMENTS: (Incl. kinds of activities, areas of special competence, use of supervision)
....
WOULD YOU RECOMMEND THIS CASE AIDE FOR OTHER VOLUNTEER WORK, EMPLOYMENT, FURTHER STUDY, SHOULD THE PROGRAM BE CONTACTED IN THE FUTURE?
....

2. Referral Form for Patients

REFERRAL FORM FOR CASE AIDE UNIT

Open Referral System—Referrals accepted from all Units of the Hospital

****

CASE AIDE PROGRAM OBJECTIVES: Case Aides are mature, selected volunteers who pledge a minimum of one morning a week to work under professional supervision on a one-to-one basis with hospitalized mental patients or former patients ti aid the resocialization and, in many cases, their return and smooth adjustment to life outside the hospital.

CASE AIDE PROGRAM GOALS:
1. Service to patients
2. Opportunity for volunteers to use their experience-in-living for service
3. Liason between the hospital and the community.

****

2. Referral Form for Patients (con't)

NAME: DATE OF BIRTH:

LAST KNOWN ADDRESS:

FAMILY:

DIAGNOSTIC IMPRESSION

PRESENT TREATMENT PLAN

MEDICATION

JOB (Ward or other)

REFERRAL BY DEPARTMENT DATE

REFEREES IMPRESSIONS OF PATIENT:

PROJECTED GOALS OR RECOMMENDATIONS: (Continue on back)

3. Patient Card (5 x 8 cards)

PATIENT

NAME .... REGISTER NO .... LEGAL STATUS AT ADMISSION ....

LAST ADDRESS .... DATE .... SEX .... RELIGION ....

MARITAL STATUS .... BIRTHPLACE .... BIRTHDATE ....

CITIZEN .... SOC. SECURITY NO .... LAST SCHOOL GRADE COMP ....

PERSON TO NOTIFY IN EMERGENCY .... ADDRESS ....

RELATIONSHIP .... TEL NO .... OCCUPATION OF PATIENT ....

HISTORY OF OTHER INSTITUTIONALIZATION: (Inc. place, state, dates)

....

....

DIAGNOSTIC IMPRESSION AT ADMISSION ....

3. Patient card (con't.)

SUBSEQUENT CHANGES ....

Pt.—reverse

PERIOD IN CASE AIDE PROGRAM .... NO. OF VISITS ....

REFERRED BY .... UNIT .... DEPARTMENT ....

REASON FOR REFERRAL ....

....

SOCIAL WORK SUPERVISOR ASSIGNED ....

PLAN 1 .... DISPOSITION 1 ....

2 .... 2 ....

3 .... 3 ....

COMMENTS:

STATUS AT TERMINATION:

4. Patient Interview Summation

CASE AIDE PROGRAM

Patient Interview Summation

NAME ____________________ PATIENT ________________

DATE ____________________ GROUP ________________

Comment briefly, but specifically, in each of the following areas. Use reverse side for additional space if something especially interesting occurred in one of these areas.

Activities (What you did and what happened today with your patient)

New Information (Facts unknown to date)

Health (Patient's physical condition and/or complaints)

Reactions (Patient's response, your mood and attitude, effect of the interview—satisfactory or unsatisfactory—and why)

5. Final Patient Summary

GUIDELINES

SUMMARY OF CONTACT WITH PATIENT

DATE ____________ TO DATE ____________

I. Appearance and behavior of patient in initial contacts:
   A. Any contacts with family or friends
   B. Activities with patient, for example: efforts to improve physical appearances, social behavior, increase her opportunities for social or business contacts . . picnic, home visits, etc.

II. Any changes in patients appearance or behavior—
   A. When and why you feel they occurred?

III. Plan for the patient.
   A. Your plan, as a result of understanding patient better and the aims of the job either in the hospital or outside, is patient able and ready for a job or home—what type?

IV. If patient is now working or in a home:
   A. How is she functioning?
   B. What are your plans for terminating with patient?

V. Your own statement about your relationship with the patient: How is patient now and are you satisfied with your contact with her? What would you like to see happen now with your patient?

APPENDIX B

CASE AIDE PROGRAM STATISTICS

Success Rate

Of the patients who participated in the Case Aide Program and terminated in the second half of 1972, half left the hospital for independent living situations, family care homes and nursing homes, while the other half remained in the hospital upon termination.

Numbers of Case Aides and Patients Involved in the Program in 1972

											n	d
CASE AIDES	51	53	54	52	53	46	42	42	57	54	59	59
PATIENTS	65	73	79	75	69	67	79	79	103	101	119	119

Number of Interview Hours Per Volunteer

On the average, each Case Aide spent 3.7 hours per month in patient interviews and special activities (which usually include patients).

How Case Aides Spent Their Time in 1972[1]

	Hours	*Percent*
Patient Interviews and Special Activities	2417	41.0
Group Supervision	1195	20.2
Individual Supervision[2]	569	9.6
Staff Consultations, Telephone Calls and Community Work	925	15.6
Recording	609	10.3
Planning, Staff Meetings, Patient Screening and Other	196	3.3
Total Hours:	5911	100.0%

1. From Time Sheets filled out monthly by Case Aides.
2. Case Aides tend to underestimate time spent in individual supervision.

How Supervisors Spent Their Time in 1972[3]

	Hours	*Percent*
Planning	731	19.3
Individual Supervision	726	19.2
Telephone Calls	434	11.4
Case Aide and Patient Screening, Patient Interviews	379	10.0
Recording, Research, Evaluation	339	9.0
Group Supervision	278	7.3
Consult with Dr.'s, Nurses, etc.	277	7.3
Staff Meetings	272	7.2
Community Liaisons, Education	245	6.5
Special Activities and Other	101	2.9
Total Hours	3785	100.0%

3. From Time Sheets filled out monthly by supervisors.
There are two Social Work Supervisors who work full time in the Program.

GLOSSARY

I. General Terms

A. acute: a person who has been hospitalized for a short period and whose psychiatric symptoms are still flagrant.

B. chronic: a person who has been hospitalized for a length of time, varying from 6 months to 40 years, who apparently has not responded to available help, i.e. medication, electro-shock, insulin therapy, psychosurgery, or psychotherapy. The psychiatric difficulties that had brought this patient to the hospital in the first place may no longer exist or have been superceded by the institutionalization process, such as infantilism, depersonalization, depression, and apathy.

II. Schizophrenic Reactions

A. childhood

While the normal child goes through a stage in which he is relatively unaware of and unresponsive to the things and people around him during his first 3 months of life, this stage passes, and the child soon becomes responsive to sights, sounds, people.

The child suffering from *primary infantile autism* (the autistic child), however, never grows out of the state of isolation and separation. He remains unresponsive to his mother. He does not cuddle or cling. He is out of touch with his surroundings and appears to be living inside a film or shell. Not only is there a marked delay in speech, sometimes he never learns to talk. He is slow and late in learning to crawl or walk. He neither plays with other children, nor is he aware they are around. He prefers to play with inanimate objects and his play consists of going through repetitive mechanical acts with a toy or any physical object, hour after hour.

B. adult

Schizophrenic reactions synonymous with the formerly used term dementia praecox, represent reactions characterized by fundamental disturbances in reality relationships and concept formations, with affective, behavioral, and intellectual disturbances in varying degrees and mixtures. There is often a strong tendency to retreat from reality, and to experience emotional disharmony, unpredictable disturbances in stream of thought, regressive behavior, and in some, a tendency toward "deterioration." The predominant symptomatology determines classifying such patients into types.

1. schizophrenic reaction, simple type

   This type of reaction is characterized chiefly by reduction in external attachments and interests and by disintegration of human relationships. It often involves adjustment on a lower psychobiological level of functioning, usually marked by apathy and indifference rather than conspicuous delusions or hallucinations. Characteristically, there is an increase in the severity of symptoms over long periods, usually with apparent mental deterioration, in contrast to the schizoid personality, in which there is little if any change.
2. schizophrenic reaction, hebephrenic type

   These reactions are characterized by unpredictable giggling, silly, inappropriate behavior and mannerisms, delusions, often of a somatic nature, hallucinations, and regressive behavior.
3. schizophrenic reaction, catatonic type

   These reactions are characterized by conspicuous motor behavior of either marked generalized inhibition (stupor, mutism, negativism and waxy flexibility), or, on the other hand, excessive motor activity and excitement. The individual may regress to a state of vegetation.
4. schizophrenic reaction, paranoid type

   This type of reaction is characterized by autistic, unrealistic thinking, including delusions of persecution, and/or of grandeur, ideas of reference, and often hallucinations. It is often characterized by unpredictable behavior, with a fairly constant attitude of hostility and aggression. Excessive religiosity may be present with or without delusions of persecution as may be an expansive delusional system of omnipotence, genius, or special ability. The systematized paranoid hypochondriacal states are included in this group.

5. schizophrenic reaction, acute undifferentiated type
 This reaction includes cases manifesting a wide variety of schizophrenic symptoms, such as confusion of thinking and turmoil of emotion, perplexity, ideas of reference, fear and dream states, and dissociative phenomena. These symptoms appear acutely, often without apparent precipitating stress, but exhibiting historical warning evidence, and they are often accompanied by either excitement or depression. The symptoms often clear in a matter of weeks, although there is a tendency for them to recur. Cases usually are grouped here in the first, or an early, attack. If the reaction subsequently progresses, it ordinarily crystallizes into one of the other definable reaction types.
 chronic undifferentiated type
 When the reaction cannot be classified in any of the more clearly defined types because of the mixed symptomatology, it will be placed in this group. Patients presenting definite schizophrenic thought, affect and behavior beyond that of the schizoid personality, but not classifiable as any other type of schizophrenic reaction, will also be placed in this group. This includes the so-called "latent," "incipient," and "pre-psychotic" schizophrenic reactions.
6. schizophrenic reaction, schizo-affective type
 This category is intended for those cases showing significant admixtures of schizophrenic and affective reactions. The mental content may be predominantly schizophrenic, with pronounced elation or depression. Cases may show predominantly affective changes with schizophrenic-like thinking or bizarre behavior. The prepsychotic personality may be at variance, or inconsistent, with expectations based on the presenting psychotic symptomatology. On prolonged observation, such cases usually prove to be basically schizophrenic in nature.

7. schizophrenic reaction, residual type
   This term is applied to those patients who, after a definite psychotic, schizophrenic reaction, have improved sufficiently to be able to get along in the community, but who continue to show recognizable residual disturbances of thinking, affectivity, and/or behavior.
   Most of these patients are placed in nursing homes or simply discharged to the community.

These definitions are based largely on material to be found in:

Diagnostic and Statistical Manual Mental Disorders. Washington, D.C.: American Psychiatric Association, 1952.

Basic Handbook on Mental Illness by Harry Milt. Maplewood, N. Y.: Scientific Aids Publications, 1969.